TH
12.95

Discerning Spirit

DATE DUE

T. J. GORRINGE

Discerning Spirit

A Theology of Revelation

SCM PRESS
London

TRINITY PRESS INTERNATIONAL
Philadelphia

First published 1990

SCM Press Ltd   Trinity Press International
26–30 Tottenham Road   3725 Chestnut Street
London N1 4BZ   Philadelphia PA 19104

British Library Cataloguing in Publication Data

Gorringe, T. J.
Discerning spirit.
1. Christian doctrine. Holy spirit
I. Title
231.3

ISBN 0–334–02462–5

Library of Congress Cataloging-in-Publication Data

Gorringe, Timothy.
Discerning Spirit : a theology of revelation / Timothy J.
Gorringe
p. cm.
Includes bibliographical references.
ISBN 0–334–02462–5 : $12.95
1. Revelation. 2. Holy Spirit. I. Title.
BT127.2.067 1990
231.7'4—dc20   90–36709
                                                 CIP

Typeset at The Spartan Press Ltd, Lymington, Hants
and printed in Great Britain by
Clays Ltd, St Ives plc

CONTENTS

PREFACE

This book has its remote origins in six years of courses on the theme of Holy Spirit given to the students of the Tamil Nadu Theological Seminary in South India as a way of trying to make theological sense of their annual three-month period of practical training. It began to take shape in Britain in the course of a student pilgrimage to which I was chaplain. Somewhere on a windswept road in Holy Week 1987 I began to understand what revelation might be and the displacement it brings. Later the substance of the book was offered as lectures to the Theology Faculty at Oxford.

I have to thank John Montgomery for initiation into the mysteries of word processing; Alan Ecclestone for many things, but especially for introducing me to John Berger; Rohini Banaji, Caroline Kuykendall, Lucy Duffell and James McTaggart for invigorating and irreverent criticism; Dave Nicholls for comments on a very raw first draft; but above all Annette Kehnel for extraordinary questions and even more extraordinary answers. Also Carol, for putting up with a lot.

St John's College
Easter 1990
Tim Gorringe

Introduction

A non-engaged God is no God: all theology starts from this premise. But if God engages, then it must be possible to know him. The question of revelation is the question of where God gives himself to be known, of how and where God is active in his world. The propriety of Christian speech about revelation, taken for granted for centuries, came under question when the Enlightenment saw fit to deny knowledge in order to make room for faith, and thus covertly suggested that 'revelation' was simply a way of plugging the gap left by absence of evidence. 'Whoever is moved by faith,' remarked Hume sarcastically, 'is conscious of a continued miracle in his own person, which subverts all the principles of his understanding, and gives him a determination to believe what is most contrary to custom and experience.'[1] In reaction to this challenge the temptation has been either to dispense with talk of revelation altogether or to re-interpret it in essentially immanentist terms as, for instance, the 'disclosure of the Ground of Being'.

In the present century Karl Barth refused to follow either of these paths and insisted on revelation as a central category, and was followed in this by the 'biblical theology' movement indebted to him, but the new liberalism which succeeded this continues to believe talk of revelation to be both inappropriate and unwarranted. Yet the issue is not so easily disposed of, for when we speak of revelation we are in fact speaking of the Holy Spirit, God's presence in the world, creating, judging, renewing, sanctifying, keeping things moving. Theology of Spirit is essentially a question of learning to discern God in our day-to-day life, of learning to discern where, in the world, God meets us. It follows that no pneumatology can speak purely in the language of Canaan, for example about scripture, church, sacraments, and the forgiveness of sins. We have to seek to discern God beyond the boundaries of church or religious tradition.

I shall attempt to do this by looking at four areas where the Bible finds it appropriate to use 'Spirit' language – the areas of community, sexuality, politics and art. Where is God to be found in them? How can we tell when it is God we are experiencing and when our daily idolatries? These questions are not academic: they are the questions of Christian daily life. The attempt at least to see what it means to search for an answer has to be made, for on it hangs our response to all of the most crucial political and ethical problems with which we are faced. What we have to attempt to do is to learn to name the name of God, however stumblingly, amidst the complexities of our personal, sexual and political experience. It is the task of theology of Spirit to try and see how this might be done.

1

Language about Spirit

In Rudyard Kipling's *Just So Stories*, when Taffimai Metallumai, which means 'small person without any manners who ought to be spanked', found that her father had left his best fishing spear behind she had an idea. She drew a spear, and then several other spears, just to make sure, on a piece of birch bark, together with pictures illustrating her father's need of a spear, and sent them home by the hand of a Tewara, who could not speak their language. The message was unfortunately misunderstood and the stranger was first pommelled by Taffy's mummy and the other neolithic ladies, and then forced to take them to see what had actually happened to father and daughter. When they were discovered alive and well, though annoyed that the fishing was all spoiled by the crowd, the Head Chief demanded an explanation:

'I wanted the stranger man to fetch Daddy's spear, so I drawded it,' said Taffy. 'There was only one spear. I drawded it three times to make sure. I couldn't help it looking as if it stuck into Daddy's head – there wasn't much room on the birch bark . . .' Then the Head Chief of the tribe of Tegumai said and sang, 'O small person without any manners who ought to be spanked, you've hit upon a great invention.'

'I didn't intend to; I only wanted Daddy's black handled spear,' said Taffy.

'Never mind. It *is* a great invention, and some day men will call it writing. At present it is only pictures, and as we have seen today, pictures are not always properly understood. But a time will come, O Babe of Tegumai, when we shall make letters – all twenty six of 'em – and when we shall be able to read as well as to write, and then we shall always say exactly what we mean without any mistakes.'

Despite the heavy irony of the final sentence Kipling's story is a nice illustration of the fact that words, at least words in common use, arise in response to the felt needs of social or material reality, or of the corporate or individual imagination. No words are simply idle. But what, then, is the felt need which gives us our word 'spirit'?

'Spirit' as metaphor

We know that all the words which have helped to establish the meaning of the English word 'spirit' – Hebrew *ruach*, Greek *pneuma*, Latin *'spiritus'* – carry a double-edged reference to wind or breath, which seems to be their primary meaning. This root gave rise to two types of metaphor: the suddenness with which the wind arises, and its sometimes terrifying strength, was an appropriate image for what appeared to be a creative *empowering* which befell some people from time to time. Thus 'Spirit' language has a prominent role in the stories of the charismatic leaders known as 'judges' who led Israel to victory against the Philistines. To use the word 'Spirit' here is to answer the question: 'How come these very ordinary people are suddenly able to act or speak in these ways?' Exactly the same question lies behind the ascription of the power of the Spirit to those who have artistic ability (Exod. 31). The use of the word suggests a transcendent origin for behaviour or capacities which transcend what is normal.

Spirit's second root meaning, breath, on the other hand, leads to its use to describe the innermost centre of human beings, what makes them what they are, their *identity*: an obvious extension of the observation which we find in the Yahwist account of creation that it is breathing which constitutes us as living creatures:

> Then the Lord God formed man of dust from the ground, and breathed into his nostrils the breath (*nephesh*) of life; and man became a living being (Gen. 2.7).

Nephesh, the word translated by 'breath' here, is usually translated in the Septuagint by *psyche*, soul, and means the whole self of a person which is itself given life by Spirit:

> When thou hidest thy face, they are dismayed;
> when thou takest away their breath (*nephesh*), they die
> andreturn to the dust.
> When thou sendest forth thy Spirit, they are created;
> and thou renewest the face of the ground (Ps. 104.29f.).

At the same time *ruach* can be used in the same way as *nephesh* to speak of the essential life of a person:

> And God split open the hollow place that is at Lehi, and there came water from it; and when Samson drank, his spirit (*ruach*) returned, and he revived (Judges 15.19).

In an extension of this second type of metaphorical use *ruach* can suggest the central living reality of a people or a community, as in the vision of the valley of the dry bones in Ezekiel 37, and our current use of the word to speak of the identifying characteristics of a person or group or movement is a natural development of this way of speaking. But are these ways of speaking *simply* a series of metaphors for social or psychological realities, as Durkheim or Freud suggest, or do they in truth speak of something transcendent in human life? Jewish and Christian faith rests on the assumption that 'Spirit' does indeed denote precisely such a transcendent reality, the action upon human beings, and on the created world in general, of the being we call 'God'. We have seen the felt needs which give us this language in the first instance, but how does it function beyond this? To use the fashionable turn of phrase, what is its grammar? In short, it is a grammar of discernment.

The grammar of discernment

By virtue of the claim that Spirit language talks about God's action on the world, it manifests from the very beginning a characteristic tension. On the one hand it refers to what is other, strange, *beyond the human totality*, the 'Wholly Other', but on the other hand it speaks of God active and encountered *in human experience*. These terms represent the two poles of pneumatology. The spark or lightning flash between these two poles is *revelation*. Revelation, said Barth, 'is what human beings cannot tell themselves'. Nevertheless it is the bridge between heaven and earth, human experience and the transcendent, the making-known of what we truly *cannot* tell ourselves in and through events we experience and in our language. Thus it appears to be 'speaking of God by speaking of man in a loud voice', to use Barth's phrase again.

All theology of the Spirit is written within the tension generated by this paradox, which may be expressed formally thus:

God is active in the entire course of world history, creating and redeeming 'from the inside' so that our acts are his acts, our story his story, and supreme human achievements in any realm may be understood as inspired by the Spirit.

At the same time God and his purposes may be ignored and rejected, so that our acts are not at all what God wills. In this case God as Spirit reveals his will to us in ways which may cut across our deepest social and cultural aspirations and contradict the ways in which we have learned to see our world.

Because this is the case, theology of the Spirit, the theology of God's activity in creation and redemption, is centrally concerned with the problem of discernment.

It follows from what I have said that any theology of the Spirit cannot be a circle with one centre, but must be an eclipse with two foci, to use a rather tired image.[2] The danger of any such theology is that it may very easily collapse into anthropology, a danger exemplified for the young Barth by the near-total collapse of the liberal theology which stemmed from Schleiermacher in face of the nationalist theologies of the First War. When his theological teachers put their names to the manifesto in favour of the war Barth saw that this theology was imprisoned in its cultural totality and incapable of mounting a serious critique of it. It was this experience which led to his concern for revelation, a concern he learned from 'the strange new world of the Bible'. Theology of revelation does not primarily belong to prolegomena, as an answer to the question about knowing God. It properly belongs within the locus 'On the Holy Spirit'. The reason that Barth included it in his dogmatic prolegomena emerges from a consideration of what we mean by revelation, as the act of the Spirit's empowering, and from the concrete situation in which he wrote.

Revelation as displacement

There are two questions a theology of revelation may be understood to answer. The first derives from the Greek tradition and puts the question, 'How may we know God?'. It is in response to this type of question that Aquinas develops his distinction between reason and revelation, the 'five ways' by which we come to know God by reflection on God's creation on the one hand, and the mysteries of incarnation and Trinity which are revealed to us in the life, death and resurrection of Jesus on the other. This approach to revelation, essentially concerned with *knowledge*, was greatly sharpened by the Enlightenment, especially by Kant's supposed demonstration that none of the five ways could actually lead us to God. It is within this framework, and this set of questions, that recent Anglo-Saxon theology has discussed the theme. Thus Gerald Downing maintains that for something to be a revelation, what was obscure would have to be made plain. It follows that continued disagreements about faith and its object make clear that there is no revelation.[3] Claims for revelation, according to him, are simply crying 'Clarity!, Clarity!' where there is no clarity. From a somewhat different perspective James Barr shares this hostility to the term 'revelation'.[4] It was a key word for post-war biblical theology and yet it is not itself a biblical category. Furthermore scripture is not centrally concerned with the problem of the knowledge of God, which is a much more recent preoccupation.

The second point is well taken, but the first is no kind of argument at all. Absence of a particular word from the biblical writings does not mean that the concept is not to be found in them. 'Freedom', as I shall argue, is hardly a key word in the Old Testament, and yet the whole of the Old Testament narrative is framed in terms of the escape out of the bondage from Egypt into freedom, and the ethical and social implications of this event. If the Old Testament does not deal exclusively with the Exodus, nevertheless Old Testament without exodus is Hamlet without the Prince of Denmark. In the same way revelation is inescapably part of the entire complex of biblical writings, not excluding Wisdom, but the question is not primarily one of God making himself known, but of his revealing his *will* for his people. The question of revelation is not: how may we know God?, but: 'What is his will for us?'. The story in Exodus 2 and 3 may serve as a paradigm for what counts as revelation in this sense.

We meet Moses as a Hebrew who has been brought up in the court of Pharaoh, and who has therefore by implication learned to see things from the Egyptian perspective, the perspective of a divinely guaranteed immutable social order. He has, we can say, been inculturated within the Egyptian totality. The story takes us without pause from this upbringing to the moment which changes Moses' life: 'One day, when Moses had grown up, he went out to his people and looked on their burdens; and he saw an Egyptian beating a Hebrew, one of his people' (Exod. 2.11). This moment is the first moment of revelation for him, the moment when a perfectly everyday experience (as oppression is to this day) becomes a vehicle of the transcendent, when his world is shaken and he begins to acquire a new perspective. Having killed the overseer, he is forced to flee to the desert, beyond the reach of the Egyptian totality, where he stays 'many days', long enough to marry and have children. Here he encounters the tradition of the God YHWH and thus acquires a new framework for interpreting experience. This God encounters him in the burning bush, not to give him knowledge of God's existence which he might impart to people, perhaps in a multi-volume theology, but to give him a *task*, the task of returning to Pharaoh and bringing Israel out of Egypt.

Every element of an authentic theology of revelation is contained in this story. Revelation begins with an everyday experience in which someone is knocked off course, displaced from his or her totality. To know God's revelation is to be a displaced person, to be made homeless, driven beyond the self-contained set of assumptions which constitute a totality, be it our egoism, our world view, or the culture of the day. Revelation may indeed involve experiences of the numinous, but there is no emphasis on this aspect of the story. The story hastens on to the task; revelation is never given as it were for its own sake, but towards the establishing of God's will, of freedom, justice, mercy and peace. The story also emphasizes the element of *empowerment*: 'Who am I that I should go to Pharaoh, and bring the sons of Israel out of Egypt?' asks Moses, and all the Exodus stories show him seeking, finding, losing, regaining and giving courage. The secret of this is God's promise that 'I will be with you' – and God's presence with us is precisely what we speak of as Spirit. Whilst the stories in Judges speak of a far more dramatic and total empowering, albeit often short-lived, the way in which Moses is enabled both to face Pharaoh and to lead Israel, with all the difficulties, hesitations and problems this entails, is both more true to later stories within the biblical tradition such as Jeremiah's and even that of Jesus, and also to our own experience.

It was just this understanding of revelation which was normative for Barth in the period preceding the outbreak of the Second War. The question of revelation was never, for him, as Anglo-Saxon scholars persist in understanding it, primarily a question of *epistemology*, addressing the Enlightenment question of how we might come to know God in a disenchanted world, or how we can defend faith as something other than a *sacrificium intellectus*. It was the *practical* question of finding a standpoint beyond the European totality. Romans 1.18 always remained a key verse for him: 'the wrath of God is revealed from heaven against all ungodliness and unrighteousness of men.' This was the substance of the discussion between Barth and Harnack immediately after the war. Pained by what he felt to be the irrationalism and incipient gnosticism of Barth's work on Romans, Harnack wrote in an open letter:

> If God and the world (life in God and life in the world) are complete opposites, how does education in godliness, that is in goodness, become possible? But how is education possible without historical knowledge and the highest valuation of morality?

> If God is simply unlike anything said about him on the basis of the development of culture, on the basis of the knowledge gathered by culture, and on the basis of ethics, how can this culture and in the long run one's own existence be protected against atheism?[5]

Harnack gives clear expression to the first moment of any theology of Spirit: God is at work in human experience, in the 'development of culture', and we have to seek him there. But he entirely overlooks the tension we have argued to be part of any properly stated doctrine of Spirit, an oversight which at this stage of his career it was Barth's principal concern to correct. His reply to Harnack was accordingly mordant:

> Statements about God derived from the 'development of culture, from the knowledge gathered by culture and from ethics' may, as expressions of special 'experiences of God.' (e.g. the experiences of the War), have their significance and value in comparison with the experience of primitive peoples who do not yet know such great treasures. (Consider, for example, the significance and value of the statements of the War theologians of all countries.) These statements can definitely not be

considered as the 'preaching of the gospel'. Whether they protect culture and the individual 'against atheism' or whether they sow atheism, since they come out of polytheism, would remain an open question in each individual case.[6]

The debate between Harnack and Barth on this issue raised the essential question of any theology of Spirit, the question of discernment, but this was unfortunately never addressed as such. The contest with Fascism drove Barth into a corner where he felt he had to struggle for the critical principal to the absolute denial of any 'point of contact' in human culture. In the more eirenical days after the Second World War he was able to redress the balance and cheerfully affirmed the 'lesser lights' of culture and creation. Anglo-Saxon readings of Barth have continued to read him largely in terms of his earlier polemic, innocent of any understanding of its context, and as if he was addressing its problematic, the Enlightenment, in which case his theology makes little sense. The great strength of theological liberalism is its attempt to find God beyond religious or ecclesiastical boundaries. Its temptation, on the other hand, has always been a flabby assimilation to the spirit of the age, in which it is always safest and easiest to remain purely on the level of ideas. Only when concrete problems are faced theologically can we expect the emergence of a genuine theology of Spirit, and therefore of revelation. So called 'natural theology' is the clearest illustration of this fact.

Theology of spirit and natural theology

Natural theology is the attempt to speak of God independently of revelation, usually by a process of inference from experience of some kind, whether it be of the contingency of created realities, the beauty and intricacy of nature, the 'feeling of absolute dependence', or existential anxiety.[7] It resembles theology of Spirit in that it asks about God in the world, but it differs from it in deriving its criteria of discernment from abstract considerations, and thus attempting to see where God is at work independently of Christ or, to put it another way, it ignores the 'underside of history' which the crucified Christ represents. Natural theology is a prime example of the truth of Marx's dictum that the ruling ideas of any age are always those of its ruling class, so that what is 'natural' turns out to be the values which guarantee the *status quo.* Thus the theology of created orders has legitimated oppression both in Nazi Germany and in South Africa. A comparison of the way in which the two theologies function in relation to the question of human equality serves to make the point. Beginning from revelation, which is to say from Christ, we understand all human beings as equal, as sisters and brothers of the Son of Man, sharing with him the image of God, and we seek concrete political, social and economic structures which honour and correspond to that equality.

Natural theology, on the other hand, begins from the perceived fact *that we are not all equal,* and builds on this. Differences of strength, talent, intelligence and beauty are taken to validate hierarchy. We simply have to accept the facts, the way things are.[8] Needless to say, 'revelation' is not accepted as a fact. Barth was right to condemn this kind of theology, as incapable of mounting resistance to a demonic nationalism, but wrong to try and meet it purely with a christocentric theology. Christology provides the criteria for discerning the Spirit, but is not itself pneumatology. The real answer to natural theology is a proper theology of Spirit. Barth himself implied this, without drawing conclusions for pneumatology, in insisting on the freedom of God's immanence. God is free, he said, to indwell the creature in the most varied ways, according to its varying characteristics, but also in himself. God's presence is one thing in the incarnation, another thing in the life of the church, another thing in the preservation of the world, and another in the future consummation.[9] Later Barth was able, as we saw, to talk of the 'lesser lights' in the world which reflect the one great light. This freedom of God's presence is the reality of his Spirit in the world, beyond and ahead of the community which lives by the redeeming story, the church. God's freedom in fact grounds what I shall argue later is the one valid form of natural theology, which is art, but this 'theology' operates in a quite different way to what is usually understood by the term.

Human spirit and Holy Spirit

Spirit language begins, we have seen, with the observation of natural phenomena, and then proceeds by analogy to both human and divine subjects. Two broad streams have characterized Christian reflection on the relation of God and human beings. The first, again deriving from the Greek tradition, sees an essential affinity between God and the human soul or spirit. Thus Plato believed that the soul shared the immortality and uncreatedness of the 'prime origin' which kept the universe in being (*Phaedrus* 245), whilst the Stoics understood it as a 'seed' of the divine Word. Human beings were understood to consist of body, soul and spirit, a view which played a considerable role in some of the early christological controversies. Standing in this tradition, Origen could speak of 'a certain affinity between the mind and God, of whom mind is an intellectual image' (*De Principiis* 1.1.7), language which was echoed by the German Idealists many centuries later. Fichte, for instance, said that the human spirit had 'an affinity with the supersensible world which is present in man naturally and independently of the teaching of Jesus',[10] whilst Hegel conceived universal process as the realization of Absolute Spirit through finite spirit. This idea of an affinity between divine and human spirit underlay the whole enterprise of liberal theology. Wheeler Robinson, for example, in his classic *The Christian Experience of the Holy Spirit*, published in 1928, assumed that our knowledge of God as Spirit depended on a real kinship between the human spirit and the divine, grounded in the category of personality. Theology must be grounded in experience, and 'the first postulate of Christian experience seems to be the reality, the dignity, the eternal value of human personality'.[11]

This followed analytically, for Robinson, from the incarnation: 'By that new entrance into our life, *personality* is declared to be the supreme organ of the Spirit.'[12]

The other tradition begins rather with the awareness of the *distance* between God and human beings, as expressed classically by Second Isaiah:

> For my thoughts are not your thoughts, neither are your ways my ways, says the Lord. For as the heavens are higher than the earth, so are my ways higher than your ways and my thoughts than your thoughts. (Isa. 55.8f.).

This tradition wishes to emphasize that it is the *Holy* Spirit with whom we have to do, or in other words that when we talk about Spirit we are really talking about God. On these grounds Barth denied that human beings could as such be characterized as spirit. 'In the Bible,' he said, 'spirit denotes what God Himself is and does for man.'[13] Human beings have, but are not, spirit. They are like the animals in that the Spirit gives them life, but they have a second and peculiar determination by the Spirit to be the covenant partner of God. Spirit, then, is always 'God's free encounter with man', but at the same time:

> It is as the principle of the soul that the Spirit is the principle of the whole man . . . Since the Spirit dwells especially in the soul . . . the Spirit participates in the motions and experiences of the soul . . . The Spirit is not man as such, but the divine gift of life which makes him man, and therefore something foreign and superior to the whole man. Yet while this gift does not cease to be a gift, it is really given to man as such and belongs to his very essence.[14]

What Barth is in fact taking up here is the claim that it is Spirit which gives us *identity*, the other strand of Spirit usage which emerges from the Bible. It is Martin Buber who has stated this identity – giving work of the Spirit with the greatest clarity:

> Spirit in its human manifestation is man's response to his Thou. Man speaks in many tongues – tongues of language, of art, of action – but the spirit is one; it is response to the Thou

that appears from the mystery and addresses us from the mystery. Spirit is word. And even as verbal speech may first become word in the brain of man and then become sound in his throat, although both are merely refractions of the true event because in truth language does not reside in man but man stands in language and speaks out of it – so it is with all words, all spirit. Spirit is not in the I but between I and Thou. It is not like the blood that circulates in you but like the air in which you breathe. Man lives in the spirit when he is able to respond to his Thou.[15]

If we are to distinguish, then, between human spirit and God's Spirit, we can say that the latter is the address, the 'Thou' which makes this being human as opposed to an animal, whilst human spirit is the response to this address. We do not possess Spirit as an inner potentiality or faculty but are rather constituted by the address of the divine Spirit, by its 'Thou', and it is this which makes us what we are. This constitutive address of God may be understood analogously to the way in which I become an individual – which is to say through being named, given roles, duties and responsibilities within a community. A human baby reared by animals does not develop human individuality, is not, as it were, named: the 'nurture' of society ('naming') proves to be more important than nature (biological potential). In an analogous way we may say that it is the election of humankind in Jesus Christ which is ultimately constitutive of our humanity. But 'election' is a somewhat abstract way of speaking of the day-to-day relation to us of God as Spirit, of the experience of God which makes us what we are.

George Hendry has argued that to deny spirit as a proper constituent part of the human make-up is to deny the possibility of a free relationship with God, since it is in the spirit that freedom inheres.[16] It is difficult, however, to see why the soul in which Spirit inheres should be any the less a free agent than a human spirit which exists in some way alongside the soul. Human freedom is not compromised by the fact that God takes the initiative towards us any more than by the fact that God

creates us. On the contrary, it is God's initiative which creates our
freedom and there is no need of any 'faculty' beyond the soul to
respond to this initiative. Theology of Spirit is the charting both
of this freedom and of this response.

2

Tradition and Discernment

Tradition, spirit and experience

When we speak of experience of the Spirit, what is it that we actually have in mind? Many of those who stood broadly in the tradition Schleiermacher initiated – William James, or Rudolf Otto, for example – assumed that it must be *religious* experience, which they took as a distinct area of human experience, and which included all the phenomena of the mystical tradition. Obvious though this appears to be, there are actually several decisive objections to taking it as a starting point. In the first place such experiences seem to happen only to the few, and to be the preserve of a spiritual elite. Can it be the case that God communicates with his human creation only through spiritual geniuses? This possibility was decisively turned down in the second century, when the church repudiated Gnosticism. Two further reasons for rejecting it were expressed by Barth in the opening salvo of his attack on the theology of experience, the 1920 lecture 'Biblical Views, Insights and Vistas'. Following Kierkegaard, he insisted that there is an element of demand and even of terror in the biblical accounts of encounter with God which cannot be squared with what is usually reckoned to be piety. He protested in astonishment at the way in which relationship to God is treated as easy and familiar, the experience of Paul is duplicated by 'earnest young people', and prayer, the 'last possibility of spirit imprisoned souls' becomes 'a more or less familiar part of bourgeois housekeeping'. Religious experience becomes an end in itself and God is domesticated.

But Barth also wishes to say that in the Bible experience as such is simply not important as a category:

> It is an appointment and a commission, not a goal and a fulfilment, and therefore it is an elementary thing, hardly conscious of itself and necessitating only a minimum of reflection and confession . . . At the central point of typically religious interest, at the point of the personal relationship of men to God – in contrast to myths and mysticism with their wealth of rainbow colours of suppressed sexuality – the Bible is astonishingly staid, sober, and colourless. It is evident that the relation to God with which the Bible is concerned does not have its source in the purple depths of the subconscious, and cannot be quite identical with what the deep-sea psychical research of our day describes, in the narrower or broader sense, as *libido* fulfilment . . . Note also the surprisingly meagre interest of the Bible in biography, in the development of its heroes. There is no gripping history of the youth and conversion of Jeremiah, no report of the edifying death of Paul. To the grief of our theological contemporaries there is above all no 'life of Jesus'. The man of the Bible stands and falls with his task, his work.[1]

Reviewing the first volume of the *Church Dogmatics* with a typically superior Anglican yawn in 1936, Austin Farrer remarked that, 'Experience is really the key to all, and Barthian protests against the theology of experience do not remove it but only define it.' Farrer is both right and wrong. He is wrong in that it is not possible to brush aside so lightly the paradoxical character of Christian experience, its refusal to fit or be fitted into conventional, and especially into world religious, categories. The only experience of man, said Barth in the same essay in 1920, is the resurrection, which he called an 'absolute *novum*'. 'Religion's blind and vicious habit of asserting eternally that it possesses something, feasts upon it, and distributes it, must sometime cease if we are ever to have an honest, a fierce, seeking, asking and knocking.' This protest has to be honoured over against the bland common sense of so many accounts of Christian experience offered at the same period, and still maintained in but slightly revised form. Thus for Wheeler Robinson 'religious' experience was ordinary experience interpreted through a sense of life as being under divine control ('providence'), the awareness of spiritual 'values' as divinely authoritative, an understanding of nature in terms of intelligence, beauty and sublimity, and 'more or less intermittent' experiences interpreted as personal fellowship with God. These criteria are certainly not to be despised, but they lack that tension which I have maintained to be an essential element of discourse about Spirit. They lack the 'fierce seeking, asking and knocking' which led Barth into opposition to factory owners, the Nazi regime, and the post-war consensus. It would be unfair to characterize them as the theology of the Vicar of Bray, but they do involve that reduction of the gospel to the lowest cultural denominator which makes it incapable of protest, which was in fact responsible for the 'War theologies of all countries' against which Barth protests.

Farrer is right, however, in that Barth, like every theologian, talks about something that can be experienced. What is this, in Barth's case? His shorthand for 'experience' is 'Word', by which he means an authoritative pattern of narrative and interpretation within which the community stands. This account of experience allows for the fact that all experience includes interpretation – there are no raw, non-interpreted data. The word 'Spirit' has meaning within that pattern and that tradition. In the place of Wheeler Robinson's four criteria, and doing the same job, we have the discipline of learning to read and therefore experience our culture and our politics, our enterprises and relationships, in the light of particular traditions of narrative and symbolic usage and of *changing* our practice in the light of that reading. The answer to the question how we are to discern God's future is, as Robert Jenson has said, 'through an act of interpretation'.

Because we identify God at work – Spirit – through a particular story, the story of Israel and of Jesus, we do so by means of historical memory, and so discerning the spirits is always a hermeneutical labour. More than that, as Cowper put it, 'God is his own interpreter' so that 'the interpreting itself is the actuality of the Spirit', or, as Lesslie Newbigin has strikingly put it, the work of the Spirit is 'to be the hermeneutic of the world's continuing history'.[2] This was what Barth meant by speaking of the Spirit as 'Revealedness', the moment by which God himself brings his revelation home to us, and in this sense 'Paraclete' (the one who witnesses to Christ's story, and declares 'the things of Christ', John 15.26; 16.14) can properly be translated as 'Interpreter'.

A more fashionable way of putting this is to say that we must learn how the word 'Spirit' works within our language, learn the 'grammar' of the word, the rules of its use. To paraphrase a remark of Fergus Kerr, 'To explain what the word "Spirit" means we have to listen to what it is permissible to say on the subject.'[3] But this 'permission', settled by the rules of conversation, in turn depends on the individual and community experiences which generate the language, not as a retreat to ostensive definition but as giving an account of why we have these words at all. This involves, naturally, looking at the social context of the various documents (we cannot simply say 'narratives') in which the word occurs, because language is part of the hermeneutic spiral which Marxist discussion knows as 'base and superstructure'. Our systems of thought, our ideologies and theologies, are shaped by the structure of society and means of production in force at a given time, but they in turn influence the structure of society. That we are not trapped in the systems which shape our experience is the possibility of revelation and inspiration.

Spirit is the breach of totalizing discourse, including wholism

Inspiration and discernment

Barth begins with appeal to a pattern of narrative taken to be authoritative. He assumes, in other words, the 'inspiration' of scripture. The doctrine of scriptural inspiration is, in the first instance, a way of speaking of how the collection of documents we call scripture actually *work* in the community, how they shape its identity and continually inspire it. But we have to press beyond this to ask how it comes about that it actually functions in this way.

Rejecting a mantic understanding which thought of the writers of scripture more or less as automata, the nineteenth century focussed on the great individual and thought in terms of the 'prophetic-personal' model. The lonely great-souled individual received revelations from God, perhaps in mystical experiences, which he then mediated to the community. There is something in this, even though it has been justly criticized for reading all the different genres of scripture as if they were prophecy. Eric Heaton warns us very properly about making our experience the measure of the experience of the great prophets. 'It must always be something of an impertinence,' he writes, 'to attempt to stretch any sort of spiritual experience on the rack of our psychological categories, and this is even more obviously true in the case of the great prophets, of whose inner consciousness our evidence is no less slight than our ability to interpret it.'[4]

On the other hand, Heaton later describes the 'inner core of prophetic consciousness' as 'intensified spiritual-and-moral awareness'. This indicates that there remains a fundamental continuity between the openness to God which we experience, with all its complexities, obscurities and difficulties, and that which grounded the prophetic consciousness. Like all consciousness, this arises from and rests on a particular tradition, of which the books we call 'the Bible' are the written record.

Commenting on the way in which scripture is used in making ethical decisions, James Barr remarks that it is certainly exceptional that 'even a sophisticated consultation of the Bible' can lead directly to decisions about contemporary problems.

> The Bible is not in fact a problem solver. It seems to me normal that the biblical material bears upon the whole man, his total faith and life, and that out of that total faith and life he takes his decisions as a free agent.[5]

What Barr is describing is what Lindbeck has called 'intratext-
uality', allowing scripture to provide the categories by which we
make sense of experience, to 'give us our world'. Our 'openness to
God' does not happen in a vacuum but is part of a tradition.
'Hearing' God speak, discerning God's will, consists in large part
of living within a community, steeping oneself in its tradition and
praying within that tradition, including non-prophetic elements
of that tradition such as Wisdom. Self-evident as this may seem, a
very different model – the model of the mystic, alone with her
God, receiving solitary 'revelations' – has in fact determined
much reflection on how we come to know God's will. The slow
and hesitant advance of conversation which the various forms of
higher criticism reveal as the process by which 'scripture' comes
to be offer a quite different model, and one much more consonant
with common experience. What one takes to be the 'Word of
God', according to this model, is the conviction or sense that one
arrives at in an ongoing conversation both with the present
community and with the past, in the shape of both oral and
written tradition. The result is necessarily far more tentative than
the certainty which mystics sometimes feel able to lay claim to, so
that the possibility of self-deception is always present. Jeremiah,
for example, felt himself deceived in the isolation brought about
by his conflict with the Temple clergy (Jer. 20.7f.), and in the
contest with Zedekiah Micaiah says, as he is carted away to
prison: 'If you return in peace, the Lord has not spoken by me' (I
Kings 22.28). The prophets spoke with authority, but even for
them the possibility of being deceived remained, as indeed it
seems to have remained for Jesus on the most likely reading of
Mark 15.34. But how, then, do we distinguish a true from a false
'Word of the Lord'?

As Alasdair MacIntyre has argued with regard to making
decisions between conflicting moral positions, this can only be
done in terms of the conflict of traditions.[6] Any claim for
something to be God's will has to be understood with reference to
the central emphasis of a tradition of speech about God. We
discern God's will and hear his Word by indwelling the tradition.
Lindbeck calls this 'interiorized skill', which can discriminate

intuitively or non-discursively between authentic and inauthentic, effective and ineffective manifestations of a religion. 'Having been formed by a given tradition – by, for example, "the mind of Christ" (I Cor. 2.16), as Paul puts it – the saint [and we could say prophet] has what Thomas Aquinas calls "connatural knowledge" and what Newman calls "the illative sense" in matters religious'[7].

As an example of this let us take the conflict recorded in Micah 3. The context is clearly a conflict between two claims to speak for God. Micah first disallows his opponents' claim to do so by maintaining that they are motivated by private advantage: they 'cry "Peace" when they have something to eat, but declare war against him who puts nothing into their mouths'. But further, prophecy fails, and its claims are shown to be false, when it is indifferent to the claims of justice. Micah distinguishes himself from the false prophets, or, as he puts it, he is 'filled with power, with the Spirit of the Lord, and with justice and might to declare to Jacob his transgression and to Israel his sin' (Micah 3.8). In this passage the criterion for genuine prophecy is partly lack of self-interest, but also the tradition of YHWH as a God of justice. It is the tradition which informs the prophet's sense that he, rather than his opponents, is 'filled with Spirit'.

Three questions arise about this account. Where does tradition begin? How do we distinguish between traditions? Is tradition so all embracing that revelation is effectively ruled out? As far as the beginning of tradition is concerned the Old Testament offers us Abraham and Moses as those who stand at the beginning of Israelite tradition, and Norman Gottwald can offer a sophisticated and largely convincing account of the formation of Israel's founding myths,[8] but of course the answer is that there is no time without tradition. A 'tradition' about God and man begins from the moment language comes into use. Even Abraham and Moses are reflecting and praying within a given tradition, as Abraham's relations with Ur, and Moses' with the Kenites indicate.

When it comes to distinguishing between traditions we begin from the fact that, as has become clear, inspiration and discernment are closely related. Both involve standing within a tradition

and intuiting its central features. The great figures of any
tradition – Abraham, Moses or Jesus, for example – are those
who do this with such authority, with such self-evident rightness,
that they themselves stamp tradition in turn. Rather than simply
interpreting, they become the interpreted (and if we follow the
Evangelists, then 'Spirit' language can be used to say why this is
the case). To make a further distinction, as the author of Hebrews
does, between Jesus and Moses, is to make a claim about both the
significance of Jesus' re-interpretation of the tradition and the
hermeneutic possibilities of his story. To say that he is 'God
incarnate' is to say that these possibilities take us to the furthest
limits of the human condition.

This still leaves us with those aspects of the tradition which
may, from our standpoint, appear to be profoundly de-humanizing. To discern the Spirit, the Christian theologian claims, we
turn to scripture, and yet scripture itself needs to be read with a
discerning eye. It, too, is full of 'ideology' where ideology means
the corruption of 'theology', God's Word, what human beings
cannot tell themselves, by personal or group interest. The story of
the slaughter of the Amalekites in I Samuel 15 may be taken as an
example. There Samuel's conviction of the need to eliminate a
threat to Israel's survival is roundly identified with God's will,
leading to a murderous war which, in the light of the teaching of
Jesus, is clean contrary to that will. But if scripture contradicts
itself, how can it provide a basis for discernment? This question
takes us back to revelation.

The notion that it is language (or a tradition) that gives us our
world can be pressed so far that the possibility of radically new
experience, a radically new way of seeing things (or 'conversion'),
is ruled out. On the contrary, we have to maintain that whilst it is
indeed a given tradition which shapes our perceptions, the reality
of things, events and persons can rise up and displace us, force us
from our totality, as the example of Moses' sudden awareness of
the oppression of the Hebrew slaves illustrates. Revelation is
displacement from our totality, and as such it is a crucial part of
the hermeneutic process. The hermeneutic spiral must be formulated as follows: we begin from the fact that there are no non-

interpreted data, that the word 'experience' presupposes interpretation. Revelation happens in the context of dissonance between our experience and the interpretation tradition offers.

For Moses, seeing the reality of slavery in terms of physical blows destroys the credibility of the Egyptian world-view. It is possibly the stoning of Stephen which destroys the credibility of chauvinism for Paul. For Barth, the outbreak of a pointless and therefore wicked war destroys the credibility of a particular reading of Christianity.

Liberation theology claims that it is above all the experience of poverty and oppression that forces a person to the very margins of any totality which makes this move possible. Displaced, we learn a new way of reading our tradition, but, crucially, this new reading links either with suppressed elements in the existing tradition, or with an alternative tradition. Moses learned a new vision of the world through Yahwism and Paul through the gospel. Barth was led back to a quite different way of reading scripture, as were the liberation theologians. The spiral is complete when this leads to a new pattern of action which in turn leads to new ways of experiencing and further new ways of reading the text. Moses leads Israel out of Egypt; Paul breaks with Pharisaism; Barth breaks with the liberal theological tradition; liberation theology discovers a quite different understanding of church.

The Christian claim to revelation is that the story of the crucifixion and resurrection of Jesus, events which were a stumbling block to those shaped by the tradition and sheer nonsense to those who were not, constitutes a permanent catalyst within human history. The cross represents the 'impossible possibility' of victory through weakness, defeat and death, whilst the resurrection is 'pure revelation' in Barth's sense, the one thing human beings simply cannot tell themselves, since death is the absolute limit of their possibilities. In doing this they set up a principle of permanent displacement. All cultures constitute totalities, and therefore to be human, which is to live within a tradition, is to be part of a totality. To be the bearer of revelation is to be called always to leave one's totality, to come out of Egypt.

From this perspective Israel's exile can be read as grace in that it finally brought the people out of the destructive totality created by the adoption of Canaanite political structures. To be church, disciples of Jesus, is to have 'nowhere to lay your head', to be continually journeying, to find no totality until God brings in the kingdom. Cross and resurrection are the *cor inquietum* which continually displace us, dissolving all claims to totality which rest on human self-sufficiency, and quite different notions of 'victory' from those which seem self-evident to the world. But this claim that scripture provides us with the narrative and categorical structure with which genuinely to discern God's purpose in creaturely occurrence hangs on christology, and on what the story of Christ makes possible for human life. It is, accordingly, to christology that we now turn.

3

The Criterion

Beloved, do not believe every spirit, but test the spirits to see whether they are of God; for many false prophets have gone out into the world. By this you know the Spirit of God: every spirit which confesses that Jesus Christ has come in the flesh is of God, and every spirit which does not confess Jesus is not of God (I John 4.1–3).

Where, in the world, is God? The question, already urgent for the earliest generation of Christians, is posed by the seemingly unlimited human capacity for self-deception. 'You will never know the truth, and you will read the signs in accordance with your deepest wishes,' says one of the characters in Iris Murdoch's *Flight from the Enchanter*. 'That is what human beings always have to do. Reality is a cipher with many solutions, all of them right ones.' Lesslie Newbigin tells the story of how, as a young SCM secretary on a visit to Germany in 1932, he was impressed by the freshness and vitality of the National Socialists, with their conviction that God was at work in a new way in their country, and came back full of enthusiasm for the new movement. The upshot taught him scepticism about claims of any such movement to represent 'God at work in the world'.[1] The history of the church is the history, again and again, both of pious delusion, and

of the power of ideology to co-opt the Spirit. We can think of
Münzer's Peasant Army, led to believe that God was with them
by the appearance of their adopted symbol, a rainbow, in the sky.
Owen Chadwick tells the story of two Primitive Methodists in
1830 kneeling in the snow and praying hour after hour, 'Lord,
give us Berkshire!', and finally rising with the cry, 'Yonder
country's ours! Yonder country's ours, and we will have it.' There
was no congregation in Wantage, one of the chief scenes of
activity, for twenty years.[2] We can think of the Dominican
Inquisitors or the Genevan Council, burning so-called heretics in
good faith, convinced that the Spirit was with them. The better
the motives, the easier it is to be deluded. The human heart is a
factory of idols, as Calvin said, determined to see God where it
wants to see him, in those persons and events on which its heart is
set. How do we escape this morass of self-deception and false
consciousness? 'Test everything,' wrote Paul to the Thessalon-
ians, faced with this problem, 'Hold fast what is good; abstain
from every form of evil' (I Thess. 5.21f.). In the community at
Corinth, which was buzzing with claims to experience the Spirit,
Paul insisted that what the prophets said be weighed, and counted
the ability to distinguish between spirits a divine gift (I Cor.
14.29; 12.10). But what are the scales for this weighing? The
claim of the New Testament, that God was in Christ, means that
God's presence elsewhere can be discerned in the light of Jesus'
story. It is his story which provides the criterion for authentic talk
of the Spirit.

All christology, says Leonardo Boff, starts from admiration of
Christ. Both historically and dogmatically it may be the case that
christology starts with the resurrection, but the resurrection itself
does not make sense unless there is very good reason to be
surprised at the sort of person Jesus was. Between the resurrection and the death and life of Christ there is a hermeneutic circle.
It is the resurrection which first makes full sense of Jesus' life and
death; but it is Jesus' life and death which makes sense of the
resurrection. The idea that we could be satisfied with the bare
statement that Jesus existed, proposed by Kierkegaard and taken
up by Bultmann, has proved to be illusory. Neither the old nor the

new quest for the historical Jesus was totally misguided, for we cannot admire an abstraction, nor be sustained, as Schleiermacher once said, 'by a mess of moral and metaphysical crumbs'. It is not just a question whether Jesus was mad or bad; if it turns out that he was 'Rabbi Average', a fairly ordinary teacher of restoration Judaism, then claims about the significance of the resurrection must be mistaken. We cannot affirm that 'God was in Christ' unless we both admire, and have good grounds to admire, Jesus. Any 'high' christology, therefore, presupposes confidence in what we can know of the historical Jesus. A somewhat extreme historical scepticism has, until quite recently, been fashionable within New Testament scholarship, with the assumption that at best we can know something of the views and opinions of the early Christian communities rather than about Jesus himself. Such scepticism owes much to the now-discredited Cartesian view that at the base of all reliable knowing lies doubt. Rather, as Polanyi argues, all forms of human knowing begin with faith, the assumption of certain premises beyond which we do not go. More importantly, this historical scepticism offers no plausible account of the genesis of the New Testament. The documents of the New Testament do not read as if they were cooked up at a 'Passover Plot', nor as if they emerge from a plain mistake. Clearly a very remarkable person, and a remarkable set of events, lie behind them. The New Testament offers us a convincing account of both person and events, and, whilst critical questions and researches are certainly in order, it is perverse simply to refuse the offer.

Within the Christian community talk of the Spirit is bound in the closest way to the admiration the story of Jesus provokes. John provides the classic formulation of this in the so-called 'Farewell discourses'. 'The Counsellor, the Holy Spirit, whom the Father will send in my name,' says Jesus, 'will teach you all things, and bring to your remembrance all that I have said to you' (John 14.26). The Spirit will 'take what is mine and declare it to you' (John 16.14). This Johannine doctrine expresses both the sense of the 'once-for-allness' of what had happened in Jesus, and also of its continued centrality in the renewing work of God within the

community which was described, following the writings of the
First Testament, as 'Spirit'. God is active in renewing human
community *through the story of Jesus*: this is what the Johannine
doctrine tells us. God active in creation and renewal is, therefore,
the Spirit of Jesus.

For this reason Schleiermacher was correct to summarize the
teaching of Galatians 5 in the dictum: 'The fruits of the Spirit are
the virtues of Christ.' To recognize the Spirit we must retail
Christ's virtues, the things which make him what he is, which
make sense of the event of the resurrection. Jesus is the *krites*, the
Judge (Acts 10.42), only because he bears the law within himself,
or in Johannine terminology is the law in flesh (for the 'Word'
which becomes flesh is 'Torah'). As the one in whom Torah has
become flesh Jesus is the criterion, the one by whom the humanity
of others is measured, something which is said over and over
again in the New Testament in different ways. 'Blessed are you
when men revile you and persecute you and utter all kinds of evil
against you falsely on my account', says Jesus (Matt. 5.11). 'Take
heed to yourselves; for they will deliver you up to councils; and
you will stand before governors and kings for my sake, to bear
testimony before them' (Mark 13.9). It is Jesus himself, and not
some ethical, religious or political teaching, who is the truth at
which people stumble and for which his disciples are persecuted:
he is the standard by which their lives are measured. 'Have this
mind in you,' says Paul, 'which was in Christ Jesus' (Phil. 2.5).
According to John, Jesus is 'the true light that enlightens every
man' (John 1.9): he is the standard not only for Christians but for
all human beings. Jesus' coming is 'for judgment' (John 9.39),
which is not condemnation, not a universal Nuremburg trial, but
rather that establishment of what it means to be human which
puts the humanity or inhumanity of all human actions to the test.
In a similar way for Paul it is 'Christ crucified' who provides the
standard to measure all human culture ('both Jews and Greeks')
(I Cor. 1.18f.).

Story and criteria

Providing criteria by which what is essentially human is to be
measured is generally assumed to be the task of moral
philosophy, but all claims to divine revelation also claim
implicitly to provide such criteria. The peculiarity of the Christian claim is that the criteria emerge precisely in the telling of a
story speaking of that which 'we have heard, which we have seen
with our eyes, which we have looked upon and touched with our
hands, concerning the word of life' (I John 1.1). The criteria for
what constitutes truly human behaviour, and therefore for
discernment of the Spirit, are to be found *essentially* in a history,
essentially set in, arising out of and bearing upon the dust and
blood of Palestine, upon the lives of men and women in their
concrete historical situations. Precisely as a historical story the
Gospels claim to set out who God is, and how he works in the
world, a claim which the doctrine of the incarnation later
formulates dogmatically. Because the criteria for what constitutes full humanity are formulated not in the arguments of moral
philosophy but as this particular history, every aspect of the story
bears on the problem of discernment.

Jesus comes into Galilee preaching the gospel of God, and
saying 'The time is fulfilled, and the kingdom of God is at hand'
(Mark 1.15). We first meet him in the context of fervent
expectation, of a call to preparation for meeting a mighty envoy
of God which produces a mass movement in which Jesus himself
takes part. It is certainly the burden of his message that this
expectation is somehow connected with his person and his
preaching, and yet he preaches not himself but the kingdom. The
phrase 'kingdom of God' occurs 122 times in the Gospels, and 90
times on the lips of Jesus. It is, as Kasper has finely said, 'the basic
mystery of his person'. 'In him is made manifest what God's
kingdom is', so that his life is the 'visible exegesis of God's will'.[3]
Over the centuries this kingdom has been understood in many
different ways. It has been spiritualized, rationalized, understood
in a millenarian way, taken to apply to the church, or to a
bourgeois ethic. But it is certain that Jesus must have understood

it in terms of the expectations of his people for a coming rule of God, which is to say of those prophetic dreams, quoted by Jesus, if Matthew and Luke are to be believed (Matt. 11.5; Luke 4.18), which think of the removal of all forms of injustice, alienation and suffering not only from human beings and human society but from the whole cosmos. The phrase 'kingdom of God' expresses the longing for God's new order; it is the name for Jesus' perspective on reality, his equivalent, if you like, of Plato's Forms. It signifies where reality is moving to, and what shape it will finally have. Jesus, said Origen in a famous phrase, did not just preach the kingdom; he was the kingdom in himself. His life and death, and beyond anything he could have hoped for or looked for himself, his resurrection, is his preaching of the kingdom.

This centrality of the kingdom for Jesus has three consequences for the discernment of God's activity. First, as Bonhoeffer put it, 'Jesus does not call us to a new religion; he calls us to life.' We are not asked to subscribe to a dogma, but to learn to love God in loving our neighbour (Matt. 25.31f.). God is at work, for Jesus, not essentially and above all in *religious* activities, but in making whole what is broken, setting at liberty what is oppressed, and raising up the weak. The good news he brings is a gospel of a new *world*, and to that extent a secular gospel. Jesus

> detheologizes religion, making people search for the will of God not only in holy books but principally in daily life; he demythologizes religious language, using the expressions of our common experiences; he deritualizes piety, insisting that one is always before God and not only when one goes to the temple to pray; he emancipates the message of God from its connection to one religious community and directs it to all people of good will; and, finally, he secularizes the means of salvation, making the sacrament of the 'other' a determining element for entry into the kingdom of God.

We therefore look for signs of God's Spirit *first of all in the non-religious world*, and then, and in that context, in the religious world. We look, specifically, for those things which *do away with the denial of the human in the present*, which rather make for *plenitude*

wholeness and life. 'I have come,' says Jesus according to John, 'that they might have life and have it in all its fullness' (John 10.10). This 'fullness' is the significance of Jesus' healings, which are anticipations of the eschatological wholeness promised by Isaiah (Isa. 35.5–6) and signs of the new future for the whole of creation of which Paul was later to speak (Rom. 8.21f.). The exorcisms, too, free human beings from the chains which fetter them, allowing them once more to take a responsible part in human society – the significance of the story of Legion (Mark 5.1–20). And the wholeness Jesus brings includes right relations: Zacchaeus is 'saved' when he restores fourfold everything he has defrauded. If this is the case, then the story of Jesus enables us to discern Spirit, the restoring and re-creative work of God, where human wholeness is sought, and where what makes for life is celebrated, which means the end of exploitation both of others and of creation. The Spirit therefore directs us away from the negative aspects of the present to the future, to the better things that God has seen for us, to the concrete utopia of specific improvements and advances, to healing, to a greater humanness, which the Spirit fashions in and through us, beginning with the present.

Jesus preaches the kingdom and love is his meaning. To be called into the movement towards God's kingdom means learning to love in a radically open way. When asked about the 'first commandment' – in effect about the central reality of the kingdom – he replies: love the Lord your God with all your heart, and with all your soul, and with all your mind, and with all your strength and love your neighbour as yourself (Mark 12. 29–31). 'A new commandment I give to you.' he says, according to John; 'Love one another' (John 13.34.). In this Johannine teaching we recognize the essence of Synoptic parables like that of the Prodigal Son, or Jesus' saying that he came not to call the righteous, but sinners to repentance. The love which Jesus demands is the response to the love with which God already meets us. John summarizes the significance of Jesus in the phrase: 'God so loved the world' (John 3.16). Just for that reason – because it is response to a love which continues despite rejection –

it must be love for our enemies (Matt. 5.44). This teaching about love is the formulation of Jesus' practical freedom towards others, his disregard of social convention. He calls both Zealots and collaborators into his circle; goes to the houses of both Pharisees and of 'sinners'; disregards rabbinic convention in conversing with prostitutes and allowing women to accompany him. This 'keeping bad company' earns him a reputation as 'a glutton and a drunkard, a friend of tax collectors and sinners' (Matt. 11.19). If the Spirit inspires the imitation of Christ, it may therefore be recognized in love which is practical and unself-conscious (Matt. 25.37), love not just for the like but the unlike (Luke 6.32), love not for the respectable but for the disreputable, not for those for whom it is fashionable to feel sympathy but for the real pariahs of any culture.

This love of which Jesus speaks is not sentimentality, because it looks back to and is grounded upon the prophetic demand for justice, righteousness and mercy (cf. Matt. 23.23). Calling to the kingdom, Jesus demands *repentance*. Though he announces and dispenses forgiveness, he is more rigorous than the Pharisees: not just murder but anger is condemned, not just adultery but lustful thoughts. The whole of life – all speech and all action – is to be lived in the presence of God. It is this demand which makes the preaching of Jesus (and therefore the church's preaching of the gospel) more than a string of ethical platitudes. Risk, openness, and obedience are all demanded from those who hear and wish to respond to the gospel of the kingdom. 'Foxes have holes, and birds of the air have nests,' says Jesus, 'but the Son of Man has nowhere to lay his head' (Matt. 8.20). Absolute commitment is called for: 'For whoever would save his life will lose it, and whoever loses his life for my sake will find it' (Matt. 16.25). The commitment of Jesus himself leads to a break with his own family: 'Whoever does the will of God is my brother, and sister and mother' (Mark 3.35). The way in which he calls his disciples, simply with the word 'Follow', implies the need for a radical openness without guarantees. And absolute trust in what God will provide for the future is demanded (Matt. 6.25f.) Such radical openness, boldness and trust, which we find in the lives of all the great saints, is a certain mark of the Spirit's presence. At the same time this intense commitment is not fanaticism: Jesus' zeal is 'never brutish'.[5] On the contrary, Boff catches an essential element of Jesus in describing him as a person 'of extraordinary good sense, creative imagination and originality'. To be original in this context does not mean having ideas that no one else ever had, but rather standing close to and bringing others to the origin and root of their own selves. It is to be expected, therefore, that Jesus' teaching will have echoes in all the great human philosophies, and indeed in the everyday proverbs of human common sense. He does not demand blind submission, but ends his parables with questions which demand that people think for themselves. He is a dissenter, a radical, one who goes beyond existing structures, but he is not a gainsayer. 'Christ is not to be defined by an "against"; he is not a complainer. He is *in favour of* love, justice, reconciliation, hope, and total realization of the meaning of human existence in God. If he is *against*, it is because he is *in favour of*, in the first place.'[6]

The kingdom Jesus announces also involves, in the notorious phrase of Nietzsche, a transvaluation of values. Those to whom the kingdom belongs are the meek, those who hunger and thirst for righteousness, the merciful, the pure in heart, the peacemakers (Matt. 5.5–9), a list which echoes those who are promised good news in Isaiah 61, who were those of no account. Another group with no importance in Jesus' society, children, are given emphatic prominence. When the disciples indignantly keep children away from Jesus he tells them 'Truly, I say to you, whoever does not receive the kingdom of God like a child shall not enter it' (Mark 10.15). Those who are called, and those with whom Jesus keeps table-fellowship, are, as we have seen, very often despised groups. Jesus' disciples have to learn these new values for themselves, and when they dispute their place in the party hierarchy Jesus tells them: 'You know that those who are supposed to rule over the Gentiles lord it over them, and their great men exercise authority over them. But it shall not be so amongst you; but whoever would be great amongst you must be your servant, and whoever would be first among you must be slave of all' (Mark 10.42–44). This '*it shall not be so amongst you*', which John characterizes as opposition to the 'world' and Paul as opposition to the 'flesh', is therefore a fundamental mark of the Spirit's presence and activity.

Unlike earthly kingdoms, God's kingdom grows in silence and obscurity, and ultimately through crucifixion, and not in propaganda, conquest and majesty: this is the message of the so-called 'parables of growth', the seed scattered broadcast, only some of which falls on good ground, or the mustard seed, the smallest of seeds. In describing Jesus' death as the weakness which is in fact strength, Paul highlights the fact that it sums up the entire character of Jesus' ministry, and therefore of the nature of the kingdom. Again, such 'weakness' and 'folly', the weakness and folly of the El Salvador martyrs, for instance, will be fundamental marks of the presence of God's Spirit.

Jesus' proclamation of the kingdom led him to the cross: he dies as a messianic pretender. His death marks both obedience to God's will, self-giving to the limits of what is possible for human beings, namely to death, but also protest against suffering as signs of the Spirit's presence. 'In the days of his flesh,' wrote the author to the Hebrews, 'Jesus offered up prayers and supplications, with loud cries and tears, to him who was able to save him from death, and he was heard for his godly fear. Although he was a Son, he learned obedience through what he suffered, and being made perfect became a source of salvation to all who obey him' (Heb. 5.7–9). The death of Jesus was neither suicide nor accident. According to Matthew and Luke, Jesus himself compared his coming death to what happened to the prophets, thus making the point that his death was an instance of what happens to a real commitment to God's truth in a world which opposes it (Matt. 23.37 = Luke 13.34). 'This death is the form in which the Kingdom of God exists under the conditions of this age, the Kingdom of God in human powerlessness, wealth in poverty, love in desolation, abundance in emptiness, and life in death.'[7]

The story of the martyrs, which continues today in Latin America, where there have been more martyrs in the past twenty years than there were in the first three hundred years of the church's existence, is the tracing of the contest between obedience to God's truth and the idols. At the same time the centrality of the crucifixion to the Christian story is not a validation of suffering as such, as if masochism was part of the gospel. As the arbitrary and unjust death of one who loves and who comes to give life, a death brought about by conspiracy, it is rather a protest against all such deaths. The Spirit of God is therefore known in the choice of life against death, in the protest against all forces which 'crucify'.

The resurrection of Jesus is in part the legitimation of his person and message, of the radical freedom and openness which the Gospels set before us. But more than that, it is the mark of Jesus' engagement with the freedom of God, of his trust in the One who is Lord over all creaturely process. As Hebrews presents him, Jesus is the 'man of faith'. 'Faith . . . is the power to say Yes and Amen to God as God is discovered through life by existing with and basing oneself on God as the absolute meaning of all things . . . Faith was Jesus' way of life.'[8] To have 'Easter faith', we can say, is to stake one's life on the promise that with God all things are possible. Jesus had such an 'Easter faith' before Easter. As the manifestation of God's creative and victorious freedom the resurrection marks world process as fundamentally open, and therefore hopeful. Christian life as life founded on the act of God's freedom is also life lived as an echo of that freedom, freedom from death, sin and the law, as Paul describes it, and such freedom is a fundamental mark of the Spirit's presence.

But the resurrection is not simply the legitimation of Jesus. The church lives not just by his story but in his risen presence. Resurrection is not only a past event but also a present reality, and this in three ways. First, Christ is said to have risen not so much into the kerygma as into the liturgy. It is the Risen Christ whom both the community and individual believers pray to, worship and adore.

Secondly, there is the re-creation of individual and corporate life out of tragedy and failure, the continuance of hope where everything seems to call for despair, which is what Harry Williams has wanted to call 'true resurrection'. If this is the case, then the Spirit can be recognized in all those situations of betrayal and despair which are redeemed by forgiveness and hopefulness. Because the hope engendered is hope in the risen and present Christ it is not hope for an other-worldly future but for new life here and now. 'Christian hope is loyal to the earth.' It is this point that Jon Sobrino has been most concerned to emphasize. Even as the Risen Lord, he argues, Jesus remains 'the way', an illustration of the path we must follow. Exclusive attention to the resurrection can mean that Christianity becomes a cult indistinguishable from any other. Rather, we have to remember that the resurrection is the endorsement of the life of the *historical* Jesus.[9] The resurrection then becomes the ground of hope in those who believe, hope that, as Horkheimer characterized it, in a phrase made famous by Moltmann, the murderer should not triumph over his victim, but also hope for the final transfiguration of the whole of reality.

Connected with this is the importance of the resurrection of the *body*. The body belongs to the Lord and the Lord to the body, says Paul (I Cor. 6.13). We therefore glorify God in our body (I Cor. 6.20) or serve God with our body (Rom. 12.1f.). The Spirit is not an idealist but a realist and must be sought 'amongst the bulks of actual things', in the realms of the political and sexual, personal and economic, and in the materiality of art.

The Spirit is the Spirit of Christ, but this does not mean that to recognize God in the world is to look for those who believe in Christ, but that we look for those whose lives resemble his, and who thus show that they have the 'mind of Christ'. To have 'the mind of Christ' means

> to be, like him, unselfish; to feel with others and identify with them; to persevere until the end in love, in faith, in goodness of the human heart. It is not to fear being critical, challenging a religious or social situation that does not humanize human beings nor make them free for others and for God. It is to have the courage to be liberal and at the same time maintain good sense; to use creative imagination; be faithful to the laws that foster an atmosphere of love and human comprehension.[10]

We 'discern' God's Spirit, therefore, in Christ-likeness, rather than in confession, for it was a fundamental point of Jesus' own preaching that confession might be empty (Matt. 7.21). This does not mean that confession is unimportant, that the church does not have a crucial role to play in its work of evangelization, spreading the gospel, telling the story of Jesus to all nations and in all cultures. Of course it has precisely such a role, and the Spirit enables that, but wherever the church goes with its preaching, the Spirit has already been before. Indeed it is this 'prevenient' work of the Spirit which enables the hearing of the gospel at all.

In order to discern the Spirit at work we turn to the story of Jesus. Does this mean that Jesus himself was essentially shaped and formed by the Spirit? Should we be led by the fact that the fruits of the Spirit are the virtues of Christ to think in terms of a Spirit christology?

A Spirit christology?

The first half of the fifth century witnessed a conflict between the theological schools of Antioch and Alexandria which we can understand in terms of differing suggestions about how modest christological proposals need to be. A currently prevalent, and in my view substantially correct, understanding of Chalcedon is that it restricts itself to recommendations about *language*. The even-handed phrases of the Definition – the Same perfect in Godhead, the Same perfect in manhood, truly God and truly man . . . *homoousios* with the Father as to his Godhead, and the same *homoousios* with us as to his manhood – in effect make the point that if we wish to talk about Jesus in a way that does justice both to the picture we have in the New Testament, and to the community's experience in worship, then we have to use the language of both divinity and humanity. These two sets of language cannot be elided in either direction. God and man are, *totaliter aliter*, and yet it must be affirmed of the one subject Jesus of Nazareth not only that he is a human being but also that the reality of God is to be encountered in him.

Faced with this necessity, the Antiochenes felt the need of metaphysical modesty. Their strategy was to stress the uniqueness of this event, to ask for a particular kind of language to talk about it. Thus, they said, we know of a union of substances in God, and of natures in creatures, but in Jesus there is an entirely peculiar kind of union, the union of *prosopa* or individuating characteristics. 'Christ' is the name we use to talk of the subject of this unique union, and we cannot speculate on the manner of its uniqueness. The Alexandrian theologians, on the other hand, were from the start less modest. The presupposition from which they began was a tradition which saw a fundamental kinship between the human rational faculty or *nous* and the Logos. Warned off their immediate instinct, which was to say that in Jesus the Logos simply took the place of the rational faculty, they advanced to the idea of the union of the two *hypostases*, what makes God God and what makes the human human, in Jesus. Their concern was always to advance beyond the two sets of language to understand *how* Jesus was both God and human. Their temptation was always to 'monophysitism', affirming one nature, somehow swallowing up the human in the divine.

Antioch

Both of these tendencies are present in contemporary christologies. There are many who are content to talk of the 'grammar' of incarnation, or of doctrine as 'second-order discourse'. On the other hand we now have fifth-century monophysitism stood on its head, with the human nature taking over the divine. A prominent way of doing this is through the so-called Spirit christology.

The connection between Spirit and Jesus has its roots, as the title 'Christ' makes plain, in the idea of messiahship. The first Isaiah prophesied that

> There shall come forth a shoot from the stump of Jesse, and a branch shall grow out of his roots. And the Spirit of the Lord shall rest upon him, the spirit of wisdom and understanding, the spirit of counsel and might, the spirit of knowledge and the fear of the Lord (Isa. 11.1f.).

A later oracle from the so-called 'Third Isaiah' was taken up by Jesus himself, according to Luke:

> The Spirit of the Lord God is upon me, because the Lord has anointed me to bring good tidings to the afflicted; he has sent me

to bind up the brokenhearted, to proclaim liberty to the captives, and the opening of the prison to those who are bound; to proclaim the year of the Lord's favour, and the day of vengeance of our God. (Isa. 61.1f. = Luke 4.18f.)

The story of the descent of the Spirit at Jesus' baptism (Mark 1.10) may well be a reflection on these prophetic passages, a way of saying that in him the one who was promised has finally come. Matthew links the healings of Jesus with another promise that the Spirit will rest on 'my Servant' in the second Isaiah (Matt. 12.15f. = Isa. 42.1–4). The connection between Jesus and the Spirit in these passages identifies him as 'the coming One', but might still be understood in terms of a prophetic figure, 'on whom God's Spirit rests'.

We go further with the idea that Jesus is raised from the dead 'in the power of the Spirit' (Rom. 1.4; 8.11; I Tim. 3.16), and that therefore he becomes a 'living Spirit' (I Cor. 15.45). All further reflection on the relation between Jesus and the Spirit flows from here. 'In the Spirit' Jesus is Lord and head of the church as his body (Rom. 12.4; I Cor. 12.4–13). Through him we have hope, 'and hope does not disappoint us, because God's love has been poured into our hearts through the Holy Spirit which has been given to us' (Rom. 5.2–5). Because salvation comes from Jesus, we can say that Jesus is not only the bearer but the bestower of the Spirit (Luke 24.49; John 15.26; 20.22; Rom.8.9; Phil.1.19; Gal.4.6). There are moments of apparent identification of Spirit and Christ in the New Testament: for Paul 'in Christ' and 'in the Spirit' seem more or less equivalent expressions, and he can roundly say 'the Lord is the Spirit' (II Cor. 3.17). But at the same time no one can say that Jesus is Lord except by the Spirit (I Cor. 12.3), whilst for John the function of the Spirit is to bring Christ to remembrance (John 14.26; 16.13). The idea of the birth stories, that Jesus is conceived and formed by the Spirit (Matt. 1.18,20; Luke 1.35) is in the same way a means of expressing both the total identification between the man Jesus and God's outreach as Spirit, and yet their distinction.

The connection between Jesus and the Spirit did suggest to
some early theologians that Jesus was no more than a Spirit-
inspired man, but this option was quickly rejected as incompatible with the church's faith and life. It began to reappear under
the impact first of the humanism of the Renaissance, and then of
the scepticism of the Enlightenment, which experienced acute
embarrassment at affirming the kind of concrete engagement of
God with the world that incarnation implied. With the growing
importance of the need to respect and make sense of other
religious traditions and therefore other great religious leaders,
Spirit christologies have once again become important. A recent
and lucid statement of such a position can be found in a well-
known article by Geoffrey Lampe and in his book *God as
Spirit*.[11] Lampe can appeal against the supposed orthodoxy of
incarnational christologies to the fact that Paul seems to make
no functional difference between the Spirit on the one hand and
the risen and present Christ on the other. More important for
Lampe than the New Testament evidence, however, is the
argument that God's Spirit may possess someone and in some
measure unite their personality to God, not as the diminution of
their humanity but as its raising to its fullest potential. Possessed
by the Spirit a person may be divinely motivated and act
divinely.

If the relation of Spirit to manhood in Christ is conceived of in
terms of possession rather than incarnation, Lampe wants to
argue, then it becomes possible to assert that Christ reveals both
the nature of God and also the perfection of humanity. Jesus is
God 'adverbially', which means that by the mutual interaction of
the Spirit's influence and the free response of the human spirit,
such a unity of will and operation was established between Jesus
and God that in all his actions Jesus acts divinely. In *his* teaching,
healing, judging, forgiving and rebuking, *God* teaches, heals,
judges, forgives and rebukes without infringing the freedom and
responsibility of the human subject. A fundamental difference
between Christ and others, Lampe believes, is incompatible either
with Jesus' true humanity or with the faith and hope of Christians
that they are indwelt by his Spirit. His uniqueness lies in the fact

that it is through the closeness of the union of God's Spirit with *his* personality that others can be brought into a union which is like, but not equal to, his own. The finality of Christ rests in the fact that it is through him, by reference to his disclosure of divine judgment and mercy and love, that they are able to recognize and evaluate the continuing communication of God through the Spirit – in other words, his finality is the fact that he is the criterion for our talk about God.

Lampe's account of the interaction of God's Spirit with the spirit of Jesus is entirely admirable, but the use he makes of it represents, however inadvertently, a regression to Feuerbach. Lampe recognizes that what the Holy Spirit does amongst us is to *humanize* us. The function of Spirit language in any christology, is therefore, to understand what it means to say that Jesus is the proper or normal human being. What it *cannot* do is to enable us to understand how Jesus can be God for us. To say that Jesus speaks or acts 'divinely' is not to make sense of the affirmation that the Word became flesh. Pneumatology cannot do the job which the theology of the hypostatic union attempted to do. We are not offered in these two sets of language, Spirit and Logos, *alternative* possibilities for christology, but rather two sets of language which perform quite different tasks. Spirit language speaks of the tradition the incarnate Logos entered – the tradition of Israel's 'messianic' hopes. It speaks about how God enables humans to become human, how they may conform to his will, help the kingdom come on earth. It therefore speaks of Christ's full humanity. The mistake is to think that it is *this* language we have to use to try and explain the statement that 'God was in Christ', as if the fully human were therefore divine. The languages, and therefore the realities, of God and creature, as Chalcedon insisted, must not be confused.

The unhappiness with the Chalcedonian account that prompts Lampe is, nevertheless widely shared and properly so. The question is whether we can do the job it sought to do without incurring its difficulties. I shall suggest that we can indeed do this if we allow ourselves first a sufficiently generous account of the varieties of God's immanent presence, which the doctrine of the

Trinity enables us to maintain, and if we abandon the essentialist view of what it is to be God and human which the Fathers
presupposed.

Since Schleiermacher, criticisms of Chalcedonian christology
have focussed on the use of the term 'nature'. Schleiermacher
thought, wrongly, that the Fathers used the term univocally of
both the divine and the human, but his intuition that something
was wrong with the terminology was sound. Talk of the human
'hypostasis' clearly referred to an underlying somewhat which
constituted humanity and which the Logos assumed or governed
in Jesus. The language of the hypostatic union and of the
communicatio idiomatum suggested a corresponding divine
'somewhat', thus generating the uncomfortable feeling that in
Christ there are two quiddities lying uneasily together. Schleiermacher is surely right that essentialist thinking has led us up a
blind alley here, though his own proposals in terms of God-
consciousness lead us up the equally blind alley of the Spirit
christology. The way beyond this dilemma is to insist first, as
Herbert McCabe does, that God is not an item in our universe,
so that, as he puts it, it is quite a different thing to say that
someone is both God and human than to say that someone is
both human and a sheep.[12]

The Fathers, of course, knew this perfectly well, though I
take the perception to be far better represented by Antiochene
proposals about what kind of language we can or have to use
than by Alexandrine proposals about the hypostatic union. It is
part of the definition of what it is to be God to be *both* beyond
all possible universes *and* involved in the most intimate way
with them. What we are required to do is to reflect on the
infinitely varied mode of God's presence which, as Barth correctly insisted, is one thing in creation, another thing in the
prophets, another thing in the Incarnation, and so forth.[13]
Now, if God is present, God is present, and it makes no sense
to distinguish, as Justin tried to do, between a partial presence
of the Logos in, say, Socrates, and a full presence in Jesus. As
McCabe asks, what would we mean by 'part of God'? Justin's
difficulty arises from his attempt to work only with Logos

language, whereas he needed discourse about both Logos and Spirit – just as Lampe's difficulties arise from trying to work with Spirit language alone.

Any christology has to make use of *both* the fundamental forms of language which the tradition gives us. The distinction we need to make is not between partial and full modes of God's presence but between all other modes and this one, which is *distinguished by being personal and historical*. The Logos christology is needed to make this point, and it does so in two ways of equal importance. First, the Logos christology is about election, as Barth insisted. It says that the man Jesus is the one over whom and about whom the Word was spoken, who was elected, in whom God chose to be present in this way to his creation and for whom the worlds were framed. To say that 'God was in Christ' is to say that Jesus was elected from all eternity as the only-begotten Son. So far, as it were, with the Antiochenes. Alexandrian concerns are met by insisting that the Logos christology is about the possibility of God being present to his creation *precisely as creature*. Realizing, properly, that the doctrine of the incarnation cannot propose the absurdity of God ceasing to be God, the Alexandrian christologies felt constrained to say how what they took to be God was found in Christ. They were thus led to insist that, in the words of the carol, 'The Word becomes incarnate, and yet remains on high.' Such a solution reflects an inadequately trinitarian understanding of God. Rather, we have to say that within the relationships that God is, *God* becomes incarnate and yet remains on high.

That this is the direction in which the Logos christology leads us is indicated by the fact that it was precisely the christological debates of the fourth century which led to the development of trinitarian doctrine. This enables us to say that God, not 'part of God' but God the Son, becomes creature, as a movement within the divine life. The second person of the Trinity takes flesh, is present in Jesus *in the mode of creature*. Inspired by the Spirit, he learns obedience, does the Father's will and teaches us what it means to be human. Since we speak of a real becoming, there is no divine quiddity which somehow has to be accommodated alongside a human quiddity – proposals about the hypostatic union were really on a false trail. Jesus is fully human, and this includes his being inspired by the Spirit (the legitimate insistence of the Spirit christology). But he is also fully God, because God can be present as creature – he is not the prisoner of his transcendence as Barth puts it. In constructing a christology, we cannot eliminate Logos language in favour exclusively of Spirit language – this is an equally false trail which is inescapably reductionist. The function of Logos language is, as the Alexandrines correctly saw, to insist on Jesus' divinity, but to do this is not to say (how could it be!) that for someone to be fully human is for them to be God for us, or to be God 'adverbially', but that God chose to be present as creature, as human, precisely in him. The Word *became flesh* within what Moltmann calls 'the trinitarian history of God'. The divinity of Jesus is the election and sending of the Son, the fact that in this human being part of the divine history is acted out. The possibility of this being so lies in the freedom of God's immanence which, as Barth says, is the way we must understand his transcendence, and it is that mystery to which the incarnation finally refers us.

Lampe recognizes that the crucial question to put to the Spirit christology he proposes is the same question which was raised in the third and fourth centuries, namely whether, in worship, Christians encounter God the Spirit who was at work in Jesus, or whether rather it is Jesus of Nazareth who meets them from the other side of death. Needless to say this is not a question which can be settled by competing claims of religious experience, nor by simple appeals to the New Testament evidence. It is rather a matter of the continuing evaluation of the story of Jesus as it bears on human history through the church. The church has lived and still lives through worship in the presence of the Risen Christ, and the proof of the truth or otherwise of its claims for Jesus is precisely what Lessing said it was in his fable of the three rings – namely whether its telling and living out of the story gives life to the world. The issue between Lampe and those who hold to a more incarnational christology is whether we live by the story of human *possibility*, enabled by grace, or whether we live by the story of divine involvement and suffering. Of course the question is which of these two accounts is true, but this is not independent of the question which of the two accounts gives life to the world. Lessing was proposing an authentically scriptural form of verification in suggesting that truth is what makes for life.

The claim that Jesus' story enables us to discern the presence of God in the world entails a permanent commitment to the most strenuous exegetical labour. That communities steeped in the biblical writings, like Calvin's Geneva, for example, should still so mistake the spirit of the crucified Jesus as to burn people in his name is a terrible warning of the power of ideology to subvert the story. Looking back over a period when the gospel had been claimed by competing ideologies, and used to justify the butchering of hundreds of thousands of people, the thinkers of the Enlightenment proposed to bring everything before the bar of reason, but the Reason of the American and French revolutions all too soon proved to serve powerful class, national, racial and other group interests – Marx put the word 'ideology' on the map precisely to make this point. If religious fanaticism directs us to reason, then theological reason in turn directs us back to the disturbing story of Jesus 'the Christ', that is, the one who sought to give flesh to the hopes and longings of human beings for wholeness and an end of all alienation. In his story we recognize a 'christic structure': 'Every time a human being opens to God and the other, wherever true love exists and egoism is surpassed, when human beings seek justice, reconciliation, and forgiveness, there we have true Christianity and the christic structure emerges within human history.'[14] This emergence is the history of God with the world, the history of Spirit.

To map this emergence and this history we turn, now, not primarily to religion, or to the church as the bearer of Christ's story, but to those human structures, relationships and activities where the Spirit is ahead of the church, and yet where the Spirit's work of judgment, purification and reconciliation is accomplished precisely through the church. Where is God in a world 'groaning' for redemption? It is the story of Jesus which enables us to discriminate between the sublimated embodiment of all sorts of human claims, all of which lay claim to 'Spirit', and those activities where God is truly present.

4

The Spirit and Freedom

Theology and politics

One of the most significant ways in which humans differ from other animals is that community is not given to them but has to be created. The attempt to fashion community is what we call 'politics': this is the beginning of Aristotle's political reflection. Politics is rooted in human speech, says Aristotle, the purpose of which is to express 'what is advantageous and what harmful, what is just and what unjust' (*Politics*, Book I, 1253a). An association of living beings possessed of this gift makes a household and a state, which, though it originates in the struggle for survival, 'continues to exist for the sake of the good life'. The good life is life in which we are neither driven by necessity nor constrained by fear, in which there is sufficient leisure for activities which do not actually feed and clothe us but in which we find fulfilment, and sufficient peace, security and prosperity in which to pursue them. The English journalist and commentator John Arlott once remarked that it was the return to the triviality of Test cricket after the Second World War, when people could care passionately about things which were essentially unimportant, that marked a return to civilized values. The aim of all politics is to make the good life possible, and this entails not only the quest for, but also restrictions on, freedom. On the one hand the self-realization which human beings seek demands self-determination for the community to which they belong: this has been the experience of all colonial peoples in the present century, but already finds paradigmatic expression in the story of the Exodus. Moses asks Pharaoh to let the people of Israel go so that they can worship God in their own way – in other words, so that they can give expression to their own particular religion and culture, and not have it hemmed in by Egyptian demands and confined within an Egyptian world-view.

Freedom for the state or the community is the necessary precondition for the freedom of the individual, which is freedom for all forms of personal realization. Whilst Marx knew that freedom within the community structure was the indispensable prelude to the personal realization which the classless society would make possible, J. S. Mill, much more naively, made self-realization the heart of his definition of freedom. Freedom, said Mill, is the possibility of 'pursuing our own good in our own way, so long as we do not attempt to deprive others of theirs, or impede their efforts to attain it'.[1] Such a definition takes state freedom for granted but it is culpably naive in two respects. In the first case it is innocent of the degree to which in all societies the good life, and therefore freedom, is available to some more than to others. Whilst Mill was writing this essay (1859), the Factory Inspectors were producing their reports of the inhuman conditions under which so many were labouring and which prevented them pursuing any good beyond survival.

We are aware today that the maximizing of consumer freedom of choice is felt as unfreedom by those who do not have the wherewithal to exercise that choice. When do we deprive others of their freedom to pursue the good? If we acquiesce in the continuance of structures which make effective freedom of choice unattainable for many then are we not tacitly depriving them of their freedom? This is most crudely seen in the reliance of the Athenian upper class on their slaves, or of the white South African middle class on black workers, but it now has a global application, between northern and southern hemispheres. Western consumer freedom is won at the cost of Third World poverty, and poverty is one of the severest forms of the tyranny of necessity and therefore unfreedom.

Secondly, however, Mill's definition of freedom invites an endless casuistry as the public good is weighed against individual freedom. Order is the only soil in which freedom grows; chaos is not unlimited freedom, but unlimited determinism. It was this perception which led to the horror at anarchy which is a commonplace in all forms of political writing up to the eighteenth century. Hobbes speaks for a tradition of political discourse of two thousand years standing in maintaining that unlimited freedom of the individual would simply be the war of all against all, since human behaviour is governed either by competition, or the need to defend what we have, or by contentious pride. Thus only a strong state can prevent mutual destruction:

> For the laws of nature, as justice, equity, modesty, mercy, and, in sum, doing to others as we would be done to, of themselves, without the terror of some power, to cause them to be observed, are contrary to our natural passions, that carry us to partiality, pride, revenge and the like. And covenants, without the swords, are but words, and of no strength to secure a man at all.[2]

The attempt to fashion democracy is in part the attempt to discover just what forms of order are constitutive of individual freedom. We accept that we are free to drive only on the left and not on the right. Some have maintained that the obligation to wear seat belts or crash helmets is a limitation of personal freedom, but in insisting on these regulations those who make the law have, rightly, deemed the preservation of life more fundamental than the freedom to do whatsoever I choose (which is the adolescent reduction of the liberal individual notion of freedom). Other freedoms are more problematical. Are there limits to the freedom of the press, for instance, when the propagation of racist literature or pornography is concerned? Are civil servants free to divulge classified information which they regard as of universal concern? Should people be free to bear

arms? All systems of law embody considerable limitations of
personal freedom. How are these determined? More importantly,
given that in every society some are more free than others, how is
this justified? The answer to these questions is to be sought in the
fact that ideologies of justification, which underlie the emergence
and framing of laws and all accounts of what constitutes the good
life, are rooted in quite specific views of human nature. Thus
Hobbes believed a powerful state necessary because of his very
low view of human nature, a view he shared with the Heidelberg
Catechism which taught that 'Man is inclined by nature to hate
both God and his neighbour'. If that is what you think about
human beings, then a strong, almost a police state, is necessary.

It is in terms of the formation of views about the nature of
human life that theology and politics most deeply interrelate.
Whilst no political system was ever constructed around a
worked-out anthropology, nevertheless all such systems rest on
views of the human which are the more powerful for being
unanalysed and unspoken. By the same token views of the
human, and above all those which are socially embodied in
religions, bear on politics. The corporate expression of faith –
telling the story, schooling in wisdom, liturgy and praise – both
reflects and shapes anthropology, and this necessarily has
political consequences. The hermeneutic spiral runs, as we have
seen, from political practice to ideology (in this case, theology),
and from ideology (theology) to political practice. Since the
changes we seek to bring about in a political system inevitably
reflect our view of what it is to be human, every religion has a
bearing on the political system under which, or in the midst of
which, it is practised, but this applies *a fortiori* to Christianity in
view of the centrality of anthropology to its faith. Feuerbach was
obviously correct that all Christian theology, at least, is anthropology for a theology which centres on flesh taking necessarily
speaks of what it is to be human. & "Nature"

Most anthropologies have the effect of making some more
equal, and therefore more free, than others – men more than
women, white more than black, the rich more than the poor.
Alongside the ancient fear of anarchy, and complementing it, ran

a hierarchical view of human nature, the idea that 'blood' or gender determined our capacity, and therefore our place in society. Shakespeare gave this classical expression in *Troilus and Cressida*:

> O, when degree is shak'd,
> Which is the ladder of all high designs,
> The enterprise is sick! How could communities,
> Degrees in schools, and brotherhoods in cities,
> Peaceful commerce from dividable shores,
> The primogenity and due of birth,
> Prerogative of age, crowns, sceptres, laurels,
> But by degree, stand in authentic place?
> Take but degree away, untune that string,
> And hark what discord follows! (Act 1, scene 3)

This hierarchical view, though taken for granted by Christians as by others, also never went unchallenged. This was partly because the story which gave Christians their world had by and large a quite different view of what it meant to be human, in which hierarchy had no place. True, the so-called Eusebian theologies which provided ideological justification for imperial courts could appeal to the royal psalms and texts about the Solomonic king, but these did not, after all, constitute the bulk of the scriptural story. The Israelite king was no more than *primus inter pares*, and came to grief if he behaved as a tyrant, whilst the Lord who was worshipped took upon himself the role of a slave and died a slave's death. This radical dimension of the Christian story fuelled revolutionary movements throughout the history of Christendom. Again, as we have seen, powerful currents within Christian thought proposed a very low view of fallen human nature but set against this was an incarnational theology which spoke more of 'the glory of man' and rooted the human in the infinite mystery, the infinite transcendence of God.

When we begin here, we have to accept that theological anthropology is always critical and is bound to raise the question of transcendence in regard to any secular anthropology and therefore any actual political system. 'Eusebian' theologies have provided ideological legitimation for states and governments, and the danger of doing so is ever-present, from the Left as well as from the Right, as the critics of liberation theology have not hesitated to point out. But where the church is true to itself, and therefore, amongst other things, engaged in working out a rigorous and critical theology, true to the flesh-taking, such legitimation cannot last because the question of transcendence, and therefore of changes in the political order, must be raised. Liberation theology has taken up the phrase of Ernst Käsemann in speaking of this critical element as the 'eschatological proviso', which signifies the fact that no earthly system of government ever realizes the kingdom. But it is the 'realized eschatology' of Jesus' person which introduces such a critical element into human history.

Freedom and transcendence

So far I have discussed freedom in terms of the self-determination of communities and the self-realization of the individual. The possibility of self-realization rests on the fact that we are not determined by our genes and inherited behaviour patterns but can choose what we do. It is true that the researches of both psychologists and sociologists reveal immensely complex webs of determining factors: the demands of the sex drive, the social class into which we are born, the adequacy or otherwise of our parents, the pressures of advertising or of our peer group are a few amongst many. Nevertheless the reality of freedom, which is the reality of human responsibility in all its manifold forms – responsibility for our own actions, the responsibility of different sections of the community for one another, and of nations for other nations – is the rock on which all human culture is built. To be human is to be accountable, and there is no freedom without accountability. True again, fear of freedom is a profound factor which we cannot overlook, and both crude totalitarianisms and the more sinister control of the media characteristic of contemporary capitalism build on this. Still, the desire for freedom cannot be stifled. The way Christian theology speaks of this nisus for freedom is to say that human beings are made in the image of the free God. Our hearts are restless for the freedom which is God's Spirit. The service of God can only be perfect freedom because God himself is perfect freedom, not simply free from all conditioning, which was what was meant by God's aseity, but the fullness of freedom in himself:

> According to the biblical testimony, God has the prerogative to be free without being limited by His freedom from external conditioning, free also with regard to his freedom, free not to surrender himself to it, but to use it to give Himself to this communion and to practise this faithfulness in it, in this way being really free, free in Himself. God must not only be unconditioned but, in the absoluteness in which he sets up this fellowship, He can and will also be conditioned. He who can and does do this is the God of Holy Scripture, the triune God known to us in his revelation. This ability, proved and manifested to us in his action, constitutes his freedom.[3]

The Being of God, as Barth has taught us, is the Being of One who loves in freedom. What we mean by freedom here is essentially love.

> The essence of every other being is to be finite, and therefore to have frontiers against the personality of others and to have to guard these frontiers jealously . . . It is its very nature that it cannot affirm itself except by affirming itself against others.[4]

God, on the other hand, is free in that he knows no such limits, that he has no frontiers to guard, and no frontiers to his self-giving. Free self-giving is what love is. Grounded in himself, in an eternal act of self-giving, God has no 'need' of otherness, but his self-giving nevertheless overflows as grace into creation and redemption. The freedom which human beings seek, therefore, in seeking God or transcendence, is not the absence of any constraint (which is as far as many liberal theories of freedom take us – 'free' love and the 'free' market being expressions of the same reductionist anthropology) but the longing for self-possession and self-giving, in short, for the ability to love. The fear of freedom and the quest for this freedom mark every aspect of human experience, and political systems structure both the fear and the quest.

Freedom, then, has both a transcendent origin and a transcendent goal, but this is not to make it something 'purely spiritual'. No freedom which was rooted in the flesh-taking could be that. For freedom to be concrete it must have a political dimension. According to one etymology the Greek *eleutheria*, freedom, has a political origin, deriving from the Indo-Germanic *leudh*, belonging to the people, and therefore signifying a free citizen rather than a slave. When this political idea of freedom collapsed with the failure of the Greek city state, the Stoics internalized it so that it came to signify principally freedom from the things which bind a person to the world. The Christian idea of freedom has often been understood in this sense, and J. Blunck's statement that 'freedom is no longer a highest good' for the Christian because 'he knows of a freedom in Christ in which he can live even while the world and mankind remain unchanged', suggests a Stoic overcoming of the difficulties of life tinged with Christian piety.[5] The Stoics, and those who have understood the gospel in this way, envisage a freedom which is essentially non-political, so that political freedom can be marginalized and understood as at best a partial realization of true freedom, which is interior and spiritual. This represents an exact reversal of both Aristotelian and biblical notions of freedom.

The continuing power of the idea of the primacy of interior freedom rests on the fact that such an idea is essential to personal survival under conditions of slavery and oppression. Just as the prostitute needs to distance herself from her body to survive as a person, to assure herself that what is happening to her is not happening to 'the real me', so those who have no hope of political freedom need to convince themselves that there are spheres in which they remain free, where the oppressor cannot touch them. Such concessions to necessity nevertheless fail to do justice to the fact that humans exist as a body-soul-spirit unity, and that it is as a whole that people are free. And whilst interior freedom may

But these spaces – be they interior + dissociative – can provide (or be attended by S) ... in such a way that's quite Body indeed be the 'sigh of the oppressed creature', a form of opium to make present reality bearable, the preaching of such freedom by the ruling class is an obvious form of ideological manipulation, what Lenin correctly described as administering opiate. 'The wise aspirant to eternity,' said Edward Norman, in his Reith lectures, 'will recognize no hope of a better social order in his endeavours, for he knows that the expectations of men are incapable of satisfaction.'[6] Thus speaks the man who lives in peace and plenty on the backs of his less fortunate neighbours, and who is concerned that things should remain that way.

Christians who advocate such a view rarely appeal to scripture as a whole to do so, preferring selected spiritual highlights from the New Testament. It seems implausible that a story which begins with the liberation of slaves from Egypt, and a people whose ethics constantly look back to that event, should be indifferent to the freedom of the whole person. This is borne out by the connections of Spirit and freedom in the biblical narratives.

Spirit and freedom

Just as freedom is not one of the virtues, but the frame within which all are set, so freedom is the thread on which the entire biblical narrative is hung. The critical event in the formation of Israel is the exodus, the escape of Israel from bondage into freedom, the quest for self-determination. This quest was continued in a life-and-death struggle with the Philistines, and the language of Spirit surfaces here as a way of speaking of God's enabling of this struggle. Whenever the word 'Spirit' crops up in these stories, 'history gives a lurch', as Jenson puts it, and this lurch, which is in the direction of freedom, is where political experience becomes the vehicle of the transcendent, where revelation occurs.[7] The story of Othniel is paradigmatic: 'The Spirit of the Lord came upon him and he judged Israel; he went out to war, and the Lord gave Cushan-rishathaim king of Mesopotamia into his hand . . . So the land had rest forty years' (Judges 3.10). With but one exception the coming of the Spirit in these stories is linked to the deliverance of Israel from the power of oppressors, in particular the Canaanite kings, and it is in this experience that God is known. Many centuries later the first Isaiah can still advocate trust in God's Spirit rather than in the spirit of man as the key to maintaining national freedom (Isa. 30.1).

The freedom of self-determination having been gained, the freedom of self-realization proved more of a problem. The framing and frequent revision of law codes, and the constant struggle with kings who were tempted to a Canaanite despotism, all chart the struggle for freedom within Israel. As the tribes of Israel came together, the story of the exodus, and therefore the demand for freedom, became the central focus of their founding myths and of their ethics. Reflecting on several centuries of bitter experience of the oppression of the lower class by upper-class landowners, Deuteronomy demands that gleanings must be left in fields, olive groves and vineyards for the sojourner, the fatherless and the widow. The demand is based on the experience of slavery and deliverance: 'You shall remember that you were a slave in the land of Egypt; therefore I command you to do this' (Deut. 24.22).

The provisions of the Jubilee year make a similar appeal. Like most laws, they probably represent a response to abuses, and may never have been put into effect, but they reflect the view that slavery should never become an institution in Israel. If a slave cannot buy his freedom, 'then he shall be released in the year of jubilee, he and his children with him. For to me the people of Israel are slaves, they are my slaves whom I brought forth out of the land of Egypt' (Lev. 25.54f.). Richard Bauckham has pointed out that this principle broke through the correlation between freedom for some at the expense of slavery for others which obtained elsewhere, for example in Greece. Since all had been liberated by God, all were in principle equal and enjoyed the same degree of freedom.[8] Freedom was guaranteed both by a relative equality of economic resources and by acknowledgment of mutual responsibility under God's lordship. It was thus understood not from a base in individuals right to do what they liked provided they did not harm others, but from its base in the community.

Interestingly, spirit-language in the Old Testament is not used primarily to talk of religious or individual experience, but of political experience, first in the struggle against the Philistines, and then in the struggle for justice within Israel. One strand of thought identifies monarchy with tyranny and looks back to the period of the Judges as an ideal time (cf. I Sam. 8). This strand thinks the ideal polity is a democracy of free peasants, led if necessary by charismatic leaders who refuse institutional power (cf. Judges 8.22f.). The story of Numbers 11 voices an implicit criticism of monarchy, and says that the 'Spirit' (in this story the capacity for government) is distributed amongst the community and potentially on all (Num. 11.29). It is surely this story which the later prophecy has in mind when it dreams of the Spirit falling on menservants and maidservants, so enabling a real participation in the new age, a real equality (Joel 2.28). Another strand of thought, which finds most famous expression in the prophecy of Isaiah 11, continued to think in terms of monarchy, but believed that the Spirit would be given to the king expressly to enable a rule which would care for the poor:

> There shall come forth a shoot from the stump of Jesse,
> and a branch shall grow out of his roots.
> And the Spirit of the Lord shall rest upon him.
> the spirit of wisdom and understanding,
> the spirit of counsel and might,
> the spirit of knowledge and the fear of the Lord.
> And his delight shall be in the fear of the Lord.
> He shall not judge by what his eyes see
> or decide by what his ears hear;
> but with righteousness he shall judge the poor,
> and decide with equity for the meek of the earth (Isa. 11.1–4).

Such a vision is further transformed through its application to the Servant figure of Second Isaiah, who might represent Israel, in order that he might 'bring forth justice to the nations'.

A later prophet, again probably during the exile, gives us the oracle which Jesus takes to himself according to Luke's story:

> The Spirit of the Lord God is upon me,
> because the Lord has anointed me
> to bring good tidings to the afflicted;
> he has sent me to bind up the broken hearted,
> to proclaim liberty to the captives,
> and the opening of the prison
> to those who are bound;
> to proclaim the year of the Lord's favour,
> and the day of vengeance of our God;
> to comfort all who mourn (Isa. 61.1–2).

It is in terms of spirit, also, that Ezekiel couches his great vision of the valley of the dry bones, an image of Israel hopeless and despairing during the exile but enabled 'by the Spirit' to find new sources of life and a new sense of identity (Ezek. 37). Given this background, it is not surprising that in the post-exilic books of Chronicles Spirit is seen to inspire the intervention of prophets in the affairs of the nation (II Chron. 15.1f.; 20.14f.). This connection between Spirit and the political is continued in a slightly different way in the late Wisdom writings of Ecclesiasticus and Wisdom of Solomon, where Spirit and wisdom are closely identified, and where wisdom is essential for government. 'Who has learned counsel, unless thou hast given wisdom and sent thy holy Spirit from on high?' asks the writer of Wisdom (Wisdom 9.17), whilst Proverbs is clear that 'By me (i.e. Wisdom) kings reign and rulers declare what is just; by me princes and nobles rule, all just judges' (Prov. 8.15). Why is it that Spirit language is used in all these places? The biblical writers are familiar from their own history with corruption, tyranny and oppression. A pessimistic reading of monarchy, as drifting inevitably into dictatorship, arose from their experience. But, they say, there is a possibility for a different order, for liberty, for mercy and justice, for everyone to have a say in affairs, and it is God who gives this possibility. The language of Spirit, the power from beyond yet working from within human possibility, enabling ordinary people like the Judges in their struggle for freedom, giving courage to prophets in their confrontation with kings, is the language which is to hand to express that.

When we turn to the New Testament we have first to realize that the New presupposes the Old at every point, and in both Gospels and Epistles much of what is written depends on allusions, quotations and half quotations of what we know as the 'Old Testament'. It is dangerous, therefore, to argue from silence, and to assume that these writings are intrinsically more 'spiritual', by which is meant individualist and other-worldly, than the Old Testament. Rather, the books of the Old Testament are taken for granted throughout – they actually shape the horizon of the New Testament world. 'Think not that I have come to abolish the law and the prophets,' says Jesus, 'I have not come to abolish them but to fulfil them. For truly, I say to you, till heaven and earth pass away, not an iota, not a dot, will pass from the law until all is accomplished' (Mt. 5. 17f.). At the same time we have to remember that in the New Testament period the only political question on the agenda was that of insurrection. The question of how you shape and order a state was meaningless under Roman rule.[9] This helps us to understand a twofold emphasis. On the one hand the Roman empire, with its hundreds of thousands of slaves, was the temporal analogue of the whole creation 'subject to futility'. The whole creation groans under slavery, and it is this situation that the gospel addresses. For Paul it is the Spirit which gives courage to go on, which is already, in the new community it creates, the first fruits of the new order.

> We know that the whole creation has been groaning in travail together until now; and not only the creation but we ourselves, who have the first fruits of the Spirit, groan inwardly as we wait for adoption as sons, the redemption of our bodies. For in this hope we were saved (Rom. 8.22–24).

At the same time the Spirit brings with it, as the first fruit, something quite specific: freedom. 'Where the Spirit of the Lord is', says Paul, 'there is freedom' (II Cor. 3.17). Through the Spirit who broke the power of death in raising Jesus from the dead 'the creation itself will be set free from its bondage to decay and obtain the glorious liberty of the children of God' (Rom. 8.21). This 'glorious liberty' is none other than what Jesus envisaged in quoting Isaiah 61. It is not a programme for immediate insurrection, but it is the dream of a new human order, which bore fruit, quite naturally and spontaneously, in the so-called 'primitive communism' of Acts, or perhaps more importantly in the review of what slavery might mean which we find in Philemon. It is immediately after the Spirit descends at Pentecost that 'all who believed were together and had all things in common; and they sold their possessions and goods and distributed them to all, as any had need' (Acts 2.44f.). Luke's account might be idealizing history, but the demand for a new kind of life, recognizing the demands of equality and therefore mutual responsibility, is clear enough in Paul's letters. The problems Paul addresses stem clearly enough from the fact that he has come to communities and preached that 'there is no Jew nor Greek, male nor female, slave nor free' in the new humanity, and that people have taken him seriously and tried to live according to it. This leads to severe tensions about class relationships and the implications of sexual freedom in Corinth, to tensions with those who want to keep up barriers between Jews and Gentiles in Galatia, and to radical implications for the slave-owner Philemon. In each case what takes the place of the old relations of dominance ('freedom' as self-determination for the powerful group, the 'freedom' of J. S. Mill) is a new mutuality – freedom in and through interdependence. Onesimus is received back 'no longer as a slave but . . . as a beloved brother' (Philemon 16). Traditional relations of authority between wives and husbands, parents and children, and slaves and masters are re-interpreted in terms of mutual service so that, as Richard Bauckham points out, masters must render slave service to their own slaves (Eph. 6.9).

> Instead of replacing a model of society in which there are masters and slaves with a model in which everyone is his own master, Jesus and the early Church replaced it with a model in which everyone is the slave of others . . . If the Old Testament

But may be, that may be, the only space possible!

emphasis is on God's people as *freed* slaves, the New Testament is on God's people as *free* slaves.[10]

There are two points of importance here. One is that freedom is not understood idealistically or in terms of escape from the world but takes concrete forms. Far from being interiorized, it is worked out in the actual pattern of community relations. Secondly, it creates 'not a collection of independent and competitive individuals, but a real *community* of mutual dependence', replacing exploitative relationships by liberating ones.[11] The transcendence of the Christian understanding of Spirit is expressed precisely through fallible and therefore often unsuccessful attempts to create different kinds of community. It is through these attempts, as through the attempts to frame new law codes, or to reflect on Israel's role among the nations, that the Christian understanding of freedom is given content.

Politics and realism of the Spirit

In *The Ethics of Freedom,* Jacques Ellul is particularly severe on the unrealistic idealism of much Christian political commentary, so often content with recommending vague platitudes in place of the gospel. In his view, 'muddle-headed good will' such as that expressed by the WCC's talk about the 'responsible society', is both useless and harmful because it falsifies our situation and prevents Christians moving in directions which would really be useful.[12] The temptation to identify movements of which we approve with the work of the Spirit is especially strong, as Bishop Newbigin's experience in pre-Nazi Germany illustrates. The possibility of deception, and the corresponding need of discernment, relates above all to all forms of messianism – which is doubtless why Jesus kept it at such a distance. Luther's early ally but later opponent Thomas Münzer is a good example of the way in which enthusiasm can co-opt the Spirit in a disastrous way. In response to Münzer's assertion of the primacy of 'the Spirit within' Luther replied that Münzer and the spiritualists 'talk about Geist, Geist but kick away the very bridge by which the

Holy Spirit can come, namely the outward ordinances of God like the bodily science of baptism and the preached Word of God'. Münzer convinced his army that the Spirit was with them, and they were singing 'Come Holy Ghost' when Philip the Elector's army first scattered them with artillery, and followed this with a systematic massacre. Not all Enthusiasm has quite such disastrous results, but the story illustrates the lack of a proper 'realism of the Spirit' which remains to this day a significant part of church life. Ellul effectively accuses the church of falling for an empty enthusiasm in its political options. But what are the contours of a proper realism of the Spirit when it comes to politics?

There seem, in the first place, to be two options which realism excludes. One is that we can be a-political, and simply take no interest in politics. As has been pointed out over and over again, such an attitude is a way of opting for the status quo, and is also a denial of freedom, which is to say, responsibility. To be human is to be our brother's keeper, to be responsible. Politics is the question how this keeping is best to be structured, because, as Sam Keene has put it, 'politics is love's body'. The other option which is excluded is the idea that we can have a Christian party or state. This is excluded both by the reality of sin and by the provisionality of all human structures. We cannot identify such structures with the gospel. But what, then, are the positive lines of Christian political involvement, involvement which could claim that it was 'inspired by the Spirit'? There are three: first, that political engagement be marked by hope; second, that political behaviour be marked by 'the virtues of Christ'; third, that certain specific options be taken in full seriousness as well as in full knowledge of their relativity.

'Freedom is the ethical aspect of hope' (Ellul). For the Greeks, hope was an evil from Pandora's box, because it taught us to hope for the unattainable, and therefore made us victims of unreality. For the gospel, however, we are 'saved by hope'. Taught by the resurrection, hope looks from the impossible present to the dawning of a new and better day. Freedom as hope is 'the creative passion for the possible', essentially political and essentially future-oriented. Hope for a new age, inspired by the Spirit, has a long history within the church, and is rooted in the prophetic reading of history, but it looks especially to the twelfth-century Cistercian abbot Joachim of Fiore, whose threefold reading of history later decisively influenced Hegel. Along with many of his contemporaries he looked for a series of 'concords' or analogies between the First and Second Testaments and the present. But where Augustine had divided human history into two ages — that prior to Christ and that since —. Joachim thought of three: the age of the Father, which was the age of the law; the age of the Son, which was the age of the gospel; and then finally the age of the Spirit.

> The mysteries of Holy Scripture point us to three orders (states, or conditions) of the world: to the first, in which we were under the Law; to the second, in which we are under grace; to the third, which we already imminently expect, and in which we shall be under a yet more abundant grace . . . The first condition is in the bondage of slaves, the second in the bondage of sons, the third in liberty.
> The first in fear, the second in faith, the third in love. The first in the condition of thralls, the second of freemen, the third of friends.
> The first stands in the light of the stars, the second in the light of the dawn, the third in the brightness of day . . . The first condition is related to the Father, the second to the Son, the third to the Holy Spirit.[13]

Joachim's contemporaries and immediate successors understood the three 'states' in a linear sense, and looked for the appearance of a *novus dux* around 1260. Read thus, Joachim's doctrine must lead to millenarianism, but Moltmann has recently interestingly proposed that the three states need always to be read together, when they function as a complex commentary on the nature of human freedom.[14] Thus the three Kingdoms of Father, Son and Spirit are always present both for each individual and for each era. The kingdom of the Father is what is traditionally understood by providence, understood as God keeping the world's true future open for it through the gift of time, working against all the forces of entropy. The Father rules, then, through the creation of what exists and by keeping time open. The kingdom of the Son is the preaching of the gospel of the Lord who is a servant, who liberates from servitude by servitude, and who frees us from the fear of death through the resurrection. The kingdom of the Spirit, finally, is the realization of the new community which springs from this preaching, precisely the kind of communities which arose in response to Paul's mission, and which are found today in every kind of base community.

Unlike the enthusiasts of all ages, but with Paul, Moltmann does not identify the kingdom of the Spirit with the kingdom of glory: the kingdom of the Spirit which we realize now, or, if preferred, allow God to realize through us, only points towards the full and true freedom of God's kingdom. The threefold kingdom of Father, Son and Spirit establishes freedom both as self-determination and as self-realization, the freedom of a community which has moved beyond class and power struggle and the freedom of a subject with regard to his or her project. Beyond this, Moltmann speaks also of freedom with regard to the future, freedom to continue to hope for a more just and therefore more human future, and to keep options open. The freedom of servants, of children and of friends constitutes in this way the history of the kingdom of God, a threefold freedom interrelated but never fully realized, because every partial freedom presses for what is total. Thus realism of the Spirit is certainly political, but at the same time presses beyond politics to the idea of unhindered participation in the eternal life of God himself.

Moltmann's theology has often been attacked as idealist in precisely the sense stigmatized by Ellul (for instance by Rubem Alves, *Theology of Human Hope*) but this is unjust. We have to ask how it is that the teaching of the church is supposed to bear on the political. As the English politician Tony Benn has consistently argued, politics depend on values. Concrete political options arise in a particular climate. It makes a difference whether we adopt the cynical realism of the ultimacy of market forces, or whether hope for the complex wealth of Christian freedom is our horizon. It is exactly by refusing any cynical realism that the church makes a political contribution.

Secondly, Christian political behaviour is marked by the virtues of Christ. Thus Gollwitzer has argued that the Christian must reject the methods of hatred or the exclusion of minorities; that we cannot sacrifice those who live in the present for the future.[15] Ellul is correct that means which negate freedom cannot lead to it: thus violence, or treating others as objects, cannot be legitimate means. In his view this includes the 'manipulation of public opinion': 'Placards, petitions, proclamations, and meetings may be effective but they also corrupt the man or cause that is defended.'[16] Positively, Christians certainly exist in politics as agents of reconciliation, and yet Ellul, too, falls victim to a form of idealism in maintaining that sharing in faith overrides all political differences. The experience in Europe of the German Christians could have reminded him of what is a reality in many Latin American countries today, that the torturer may come to Mass along with the victim, that the oppressor seeks ideological support for defending his wealth with death squads in the same liturgy as the oppressed seeks inspiration for the struggle against him. Latin Americans have had to face the possibility that the eucharist cannot always be celebrated. Apostasy and idolatry are a reality within the church and sometimes (as at Barmen) have to be named. There is the ever-present possibility, in other words, that what is called 'faith' is not faith at all.

Ellul's idea that 'all opinions should have Christian representatives' is both careless and irresponsible. Would he seriously apply this to the Nazi party, for instance, or the Arena party in El Salvador, or the ruling Nationalist party in South Africa? It is simply not always the case that 'political adversaries can be fully united in Christ'. What Ellul identifies as an unevangelical militancy may in fact be a sober and necessary recognition of a fundamental apostasy, an apostasy evidenced, in the three cases mentioned, by policies of systematic murder. The reconciliation

proper to Christian behaviour cannot mean turning a blind eye
to what brings death (the fundamental mark of idolatry). At the
same time it is true that the Christian acts in full knowledge of
her own need for forgiveness, in full knowledge of the determin-
isms which grip human beings and lead them to act in inhuman
ways, and in this knowledge exercises the ministry of reconciliation. Talk of reconciliation is perilously easy for those whose
loved ones are not disappeared, tortured, or murdered. It is the
consistent witness of just these people, however, that hatred can
be overcome by love.

Thirdly, love is not abstract. It only has meaning as an
enfleshed word. This means espousing particular parties and
political options, in the full knowledge of their relativity, and yet
not half-heartedly, but as a task to which we are really called.
These options have a certain framework, or direction. Part of
this is the option for the poor. True, it is not always easy to see
which particular option is really 'for the poor' (one thinks of the
numerous populisms which use this rhetoric but which are
basically paternalist). Nevertheless, betting on the rich clearly
cannot be an option for the poor. It cannot be the case that there
is no reason to choose between 'left' and 'right', nor is it the case
that politics has no ideological or spiritual content. On the
contrary, any concrete option expresses a particular view of the
human and of society. Irrespective of slogans, the question for
Christian political involvement is about what gives life – to the
poor in our own society, to the Third World, and to the
environment. Amongst a range of options or parties we are
called to seek those most oriented in this direction and then to
improve them – not to throw up our hands at the hopelessness
of the task.

This will be an option for what is qualitatively new:

A Christianity which is not revolutionary is nothing. Faith
is not lived out if it is not revolutionary, i.e. if it does
not constantly challenge the existing situation, if it is not
continually at work as a ferment. When faith settles down
in a society, when it does not seek to overthrow both the

social set up and the individual set-up, revelation is be-trayed.[17]

Ellul's view is that the means to do this in contemporary Western society is to espouse anarchy, not as a political programme but as 'a protest and a sign of cleavage' in the face of what he takes to be a general statist system. His view that the church must always be in opposition is surely correct – the church always exists, like the prophets, as 'a watchman'. In the terms of our earlier analysis, revelation always displaces us, forces us out of the totality of which we are a part. Ellul's diagnosis of the current situation is, however, lamentable, and plays into the hands of the American Enterprise Institute and other radical right wing organizations which currently dominate the Western polit-ical scene and see an atomic individualism as the necessary substructure for the 'free' market. It is not statism which is the problem but the control of the market, increasingly able to set the agenda for everything from education to health care and even the probation service. Against *these* forces, what is called for is rather a new recognition that we all belong together as members of one body, and that respect for all entails equality both of opportunity and of reward.

In Ellul's view, the only motive for Christian political involve-ment is to witness to Christ. To be a Christian is to be someone for whom Christ is the centre of one's life, and to that extent everything one does must be witness; and yet the question is, how? Is it really the case that refusal to speak of Christ openly in every situation is conformism, fear of being identified with an unfashionable option? Might it not also be a recognition that such talk can only operate on an appropriately deep level, in response to the other's questions, and that whilst other forms of talk might satisfy one's conscience, they are in fact alienating, and in no way contribute to authentic Christian witness? Is it not rather the case that real solidarity with the poor by those known to be Christian but who are not concerned specifically to draw attention to themselves is a far more authentic form of witness? And in this sense might not political activity itself be a form of witness – not in terms of the results achieved, but in terms of the love and compassion for others which this very often disagreeable work entails?

A political culture informed by hope, by a refusal to be defeated by repeated failures, by a consistent priority for the oppressed, by a refusal to be cornered into hatred of the opponent, and by the preparedness to adopt concrete options, constitutes realism of the Spirit in the political realm. Bismarck, a practising Christian, scornfully dismissed the possibility of governing a state by the ethics of the Sermon on the Mount, and advocated, as the political concomitant of the 'Two Kingdoms' theory, *Realpolitik* instead. The fruits of this 'realism' were, amongst other things, two wars, the Holocaust, Dresden, and the partition of Germany.

But if there is a God, then his will is revealed (for a non-engaged God is no God), and what is revealed is what really is the case, how reality is. The law and the prophets, the teaching, death, and resurrection of Jesus, are the revelation of reality. We can oppose this reality, we can opt for all kinds of pseudo-realisms (such as the 'realism of the market' for instance), but in doing so we bring ourselves into suicidal conflict with reality itself. We sow the wind of untruth and unreality and reap the whirlwind of destruction. Realism of the Spirit, by contrast, is to insist precisely not that you cannot run a state by the ethics of the Sermon on the Mount, but that it is disastrous to do anything else. Politics is about power, but, if we take the New Testament seriously, it cannot be about the power of 'this world'; it must be about displaced power, what Gutiérrez calls 'the power of the poor in history'.[18]

The answer to the question 'Where is God?' has, of course, many levels. If we say that God meets us in the crucified, this means not only in the martyr, in the victim of the camps, but in the poor. According to the Gospels, God's power does not operate on the 'trickle-down' theory. As Paul understood it, it is not betting on the strong but betting on the weak (I Cor. 1.20f.). Like Dostoevsky's Grand Inquisitor, we find it difficult to take this seriously. That 'real' power is with the strong seems so self-evident. We cannot accept the scandal of particularity. If we can accept Israel and the one Jew Jesus, then we cannot accept that God works for the salvation of the rich through the poor, by taking sides. We are not convinced by the fact that what we call power always turns out to be ultimately destructive. We are not convinced that the Sermon on the Mount is not utopian but realistic – about feasible and sustainable human community, community which will not tear itself apart by hatred and division, and which will not destroy the environment within which human beings are set. Like the Grand Inquisitor, we want to reply that the Sermon does not take account of the reality of human sin, as if this is not precisely what Jesus did, precisely the meaning of his whole life, his teaching as well as his death.

Revelation is, truly, what we *cannot* tell ourselves. The displacement brought about by revelation in the political sphere is to take seriously what Paul expressed in Colossians, that Christ is at the heart of all reality, including the political, and this means concretely to take our place alongside the poor, to learn a different kind of politics. To do this is to take seriously Jesus' prayer that the kingdom come 'on earth' as a matter of *faith*, in the conviction that we can then discover a realism and a freedom which is neither cynical nor bound to a deceptive messianism.

God as Spirit gives himself to his creation. He gives not 'something' but himself, himself as perfect freedom in and through the presence of the poor. As God woos and leads persons to himself so they seek freedom, for to be truly free is to correspond to God. Freedom, we have seen, is indivisible: spiritual freedom cannot be played off against political freedom; individual freedom cannot be played off against freedom in community. Neither personal, nor political, nor spiritual freedom can be attained at the expense of the other; the denial of the one is the denial of the other. The partial freedom we know, in our relationships, in our faith, in politics, is the measure of our growth into the fullness of Christ, which is our future. All struggles for freedom lead to him. But another way of saying this is to say that it is the Spirit who leads us into all our freedoms. Where we have really experienced, not freedom, but at least the struggle for freedom, there we have known God.

— 5 —

Spirit and Community

Community as sacrament

'Man becomes an I through a Thou' (Martin Buber). The I and the Thou in which human being is realized is community: human beings are as they are in community. In this being together Spirit is known: 'as soon as we touch a Thou, we are touched by a breath of eternal life'.[1]

Spirit in its human manifestations is man's response to his Thou . . . Spirit is not in the I but between I and Thou. It is not like the blood that circulates in you but like the air in which you breathe. Man lives in the spirit when he is able to respond to his Thou. He is able to do that when he enters into this relation with his whole being. It is solely by virtue of his power to relate that man is able to live in the Spirit.[2]

In the sixty years of discussion which have intervened since *I and Thou* was first published, Buber's theses have been extended, annotated and deepened but not contradicted. The meeting with a Thou (and the second singular pronoun emphasizes more strongly than the all-purpose 'You' that we speak of a real meeting, deep speaking to deep, and not the string of evasions and

this has prime resonance Hegel

dodges which so often pass for meeting) is a breath of eternal life
only because God is the irreducible Thou. Responding to the
Thou in my neighbour is living within God, within the pattern of
correspondences and relations which he calls forth and which
constitute created reality. As we relate, we are in the image of
God, for the image is the echoing of the relationship God is. As,
and only as, we relate we live in the Spirit.

That human beings exist only in community is the most
obvious starting point for any anthropology, given the fact that
they are formed by language, which is by definition social, and the
peculiarity (compared with other mammals) of the human
infant's needs. The fact that this creature is so helpless for such a
long time after birth and that at no time is the single individual
capable for long of carrying out all the operations needed for
survival makes community an intrinsic part of what it is to be
human. We need others not simply for procreation but for the
provision of food, clothing and protection. Since the emergence
of the high cultures there have been philosophies and religions
which have turned their back on these facts, which have sought
essential humanness in solitude, a current which entered Christianity through the Neo-Platonism of Dionysus, and which
underlies the teaching of so standard a spiritual classic as Thomas
à Kempis' *Imitation of Christ*. Nevertheless, both Judaism and
Christianity have in general repudiated this option, affirming
community as central to human being. A self-avowed enemy of
Christianity such as Nietzsche saw the importance of this
affirmation far more clearly than many theologians of his time,
and his championship of the lonely, great-souled individual was
bound up with his passionate rejection of Christianity as a
religion of mass humanity. But Christianity not only affirms
humanity as fellow humanity, but understands fellow humanity
as the sacrament of our encounter with God.

Through my neighbour I know God: in other words, revelation
is bound up with my encounter with my 'Thou' – the Spirit works
and is known in this encounter. The one who is other to me,
whom I cannot ultimately colonize, who resists me and interro-
gates and so stands outside my totality, is always the potential

place of revelation – what I cannot tell myself. The one who is ultimately Other, who stubbornly resists all attempts to fit him into a ready-made category, is Jesus of Nazareth. He is the Stranger in the midst of history, and for this reason the ultimate locus of revelation. The doctrine of the incarnation affirms that in meeting Jesus we meet the mystery at the heart of all created reality. This claim arises as the result of reflection not only on the cross and resurrection, but also on all the stories of encounter in the Gospels – these, too, are full of an unaccountable strangeness. The first chapter of Mark's Gospel summarizes the whole in its record of meetings which cause people to leave everything to follow Jesus (1.18), to be astonished at his teaching (1.22) and authority (1.27), and to be healed (1.34). We have a gospel at all only because, after the crucifixion, 'behold, Jesus met them and said, Hail!' (Matt. 28.9) – the strangest meeting of all. In these meetings, in which demons are cast out, the poor are raised up, and the spiritual leaders of the day challenged, Jesus always points away from himself to the present reality of God: 'If it is by the Spirit of God I cast out demons,' he says, 'then is the kingdom of God come upon you' (Matt. 12.28). Not only in the resurrection but in Jesus' teaching, healing and calling to discipleship, Spirit is known and 'fire is cast upon the earth'.

Reviewing the discussion of Buber's ideas, Pannenberg wishes to extend his personalist perspective to include our relationship to the future and to all the ways in which we transcend ourselves and our environment. He calls this (using a term of H. Plessner) 'exocentricity', which 'in the final analysis . . . is simply another name for self-consciousness and therefore for spirit'.[3]

> To the extent that human beings exist exocentrically in a presence to what is other than themselves, precisely as other, and experience themselves from that vantage point, the life giving power of the spirit, which raises them above their own finiteness, manifests itself in an intensified form.'[4]

Pannenberg is right, but he formulates the point in a typically idealist way. The 'other' in whom God is encountered is, as we have seen, precisely the one on the borders of my totality, the poor. The otherness of being which Pannenberg calls 'the life giving power of the spirit' because it breaks open the tomb of the *homo incurvatus in se,* does so by breaking open the self-justifying axioms of the totalities in which we live. The power of the Spirit is manifested in the those who from 'beyond the pale' break open this totality.

Pannenberg's talk of a fundamental human exocentricity manifests the abstract, and therefore politically conservative, form of all natural theology. We go beyond this in the first instance not by the help of the theses of fundamental anthropology but by raising the question of Jesus of Nazareth. That Jesus is the Other, the Stranger, the one no human culture can reduce to its own totality, and therefore the never-ending source of revelation, is what it is the task of the doctrine of the incarnation to defend.

Following, then, the holy Fathers, we all with one voice teach that it should be confessed that our Lord Jesus Christ is one and the same Son, the Same perfect in Godhead, the Same perfect in manhood, truly God and truly man . . .

What is this 'Definition' of Chalcedon but an insistence on the strangeness of Jesus in the midst of our history? We gloss this not, for instance, in insisting that the incarnation is without analogy, but by learning the implications of this strangeness. Whatever is done to 'the least of these my brethren' is done to me, says Jesus (Matt. 25.40). The parable tells us where Jesus, or if not Jesus, where the community taught by him, *found God.* It is not abstract; it does not establish another 'universal truth'. On the contrary, it establishes that; 'we stand before a God who is a challenge, a God who overturns our human categories . . . who judges us on the basis of our concrete, historical actions towards the poor'.[5] Community is the most fundamental condition of our knowledge of God; not, however, community *as such,* but the concrete community which exists in the dialectic of rich and poor, in which the one defines the other, and in which God meets us from a particular direction.

If this thesis is challenged by an abstract universalism, equally it is challenged by the extraordinarily deep-rooted, and still widely prevalent, individualism of Western theology. For this reason it cannot be too often repeated that such individualism has no grounds in either Old or New Testament. Thus Eichrodt writes that 'Old Testament faith knows nothing, in any situation or at any time, of a religious individualism which grants a man a private relationship with God unconnected with the community either in its roots, its realization, or its goal'.[6] Being as community lies at the heart of Israel's understanding of her vocation. Abraham is called to be a nation (*goy*), a corporate body, though far more important is the announcement that Israel is YHWH's *people* (*'am*): 'I shall be your God and you shall be my people' is the promise on which everything rests for the prophets (Jer.7.23; cf. Hos. 1.9, Ezek. 11.20; Zech. 8.8). The call addressed to any individual is always subordinate to this prior calling of the people. It is to the people and for the people that the promises are addressed, even the promises to David. Through this people 'all nations will bless themselves' (Gen. 12.3), and it is with the whole people that the new covenant will be made in which 'all shall know me, from the least of them to the greatest' (Jer. 31.34). Though this passage has sometimes been read as the charter of individualism, it is important to note that it is made 'with the house of Israel and the house of Judah' rather than with individuals (v.31): 'What is envisaged by the text remains essentially the core of the deuteronomistic view of community religion, except that it will be realized more effectively in the future.'[7] Knowledge of God may be *internalized*, but this does not mean that it is entirely unmediated through the community. On the contrary, for Jeremiah knowledge of God consists in the practice of justice. Speaking of Josiah, he says:

He judged the cause of the poor and needy;
then it was well.
Is not this to know me?
says the Lord (Jer. 22.16).

Knowledge of God, in other words, consists in the practical interactions of persons, in 'doing justice' in the community. For this reason, in a situation where there is 'swearing, lying, killing, stealing, and committing adultery' – things which were prohibited by the 'Ten Commandments' precisely because they destroy community – there can be 'no knowledge of God in the land' (Hos. 4.1f.). What is required, by contrast, is '*ḥesed* and *emeth*', mercy and truth, both of which are essentially relational concepts.[8] Again, Ezekiel's announcement that 'the soul that sins shall die' (18.20) is cast within a framework where the 'individual' 'does not oppress any one, but restores to the debtor his pledge, commits no robbery, gives his bread to the hungry and covers the naked with a garment, does not lend at interest or take any increase, witholds his hand from iniquity, (and) executes justice between man and man' (18.7f.). In other words, the context is the fulfilment of the covenant which will see that there are no poor.

As far as the New Testament is concerned there is no gospel without community. We need only look at Jesus' care for the 'little flock', his calling and instructing of the Twelve, his fellowship meals, and the prayer for unity in John's Gospel. This is not community 'for its own sake' but for the sake of the kingdom, signalized by the salvation of rich people like Zacchaeus, who restores fourfold all that he has taken, and of marginalized people, 'sinners', who are brought in to an accepting and forgiving community. Again, all of Paul's most fundamental assumptions imply being in community: the importance of the 'body', of being 'in Christ', and of 'fellowship' (*koinonia*), with all its practical consequences. 'Community' for Paul means caring for the poor church in Jerusalem, not humiliating those who have nothing in Corinth, recognizing that a slave is a brother, accepting Gentiles without any preamble in Galatia, having 'the mind of Christ' who took the form of a slave and did slave work. Individualism, for the New Testament, is not a possible option. Only in and through community is the living God encountered, but again not abstractly but as, concretely, the mighty are put down from their thrones and those of low degree exalted.

When community is understood in terms of this *process* then it becomes 'sacramental' in the Augustinian sense of being a means or channel of 'grace', a mediator of the forgiving, healing, restorative power of God. There is no pure meeting with the Thou – the main problem with Buber's work is its abstraction. There are only meetings mediated through the awkwardnesses of families, places of work, schools, churches, across sexual, racial and class divides, full of tensions, dislikes and misunderstandings. The very often unlovely structures of community have importance because they do in fact enable the I-Thou encounter, they make the meeting which is the breath of life and awareness of God's engagement possible, but it is their fundamental awkwardness which raises the question of discernment.

Communalism

As well as a channel of grace, community may be the means of destruction. 'Communalism' is the name for that situation where community solidarity is pitted against community solidarity, Protestant against Catholic, Sinhalese against Tamil, Hindu against Muslim, and so on around the world. Both nationalism and most religious conflicts may be understood primarily as instances of communalism, and indeed religion is one of the worst sources of communal violence. Is it possible for a community, and especially for the church, both to maintain its identity, say with a set of strongly individual beliefs and norms, and yet not turn defensively against other communities? Most forms of religious communalism involve belief-claims which cannot be surrendered without surrendering the particularity of the religion in question.[9]

Is religion, then, *necessarily* communal? This claim would be as destructive of Christianity as finding the bones of Jesus in Palestine. Eighteenth-century Europe seems tacitly to have assumed that it was, but the 'toleration' with which it replaced the religious-communal violence of the previous century was in practice simply a revising of priorities. Religious values were demoted in importance and national and mercantile values were

now recognized as paramount. Such 'toleration' often amounts
to the fact that we agree that the issue under dispute is not worth
fighting about, and as such has little value. Defending the
fundamentalist reaction to Salman Rushdie's book *The Satanic
Verses*, Shabbir Akhtar scorned contemporary Christian 'tolerance' and argued that:

> The continual blasphemies against the Christian faith have
> totally undermined it. Any faith which compromises its
> internal temper of militant wrath is destined for the dustbin of
> history, for it can no longer preserve its faithful heritage in the
> face of the corrosive influences.[10]

Akhtar went on to threaten either 'holy war' against the 'House
of Rejection', or *hijrah* (emigration), reminding non-Muslims
that 'the last time there was a *hijrah*, a unified Muslim enterprise
of faith and power spread with phenomenal speed in the fastest
permanent conquest of recorded military history'. It was against
precisely this kind of religious fanaticism (a term Akhtar accepts
for himself) that the tolerant indifference of the Enlightenment
arose, and as a protest against all forms of fanaticism it retains its
importance. Nevertheless, both toleration and fanaticism issue in
different ways in the destruction of community: one by a
withering away from within, and the other through inter-
communal conflict. Both are denials of the sacramentality of
community, one by a retreat to individualism, the other by
denying God in those who differ, identifying them, be they
Protestant, Catholic, Hindu or Muslim, with the 'House of
Rejection'. Must we accept the choice between empty tolerance
and an even emptier fanaticism as a *necessary* dilemma, or are
there alternatives?

The Christian church arose in confronting precisely this
dilemma. Jesus' cleansing of the Temple was a protest against
Jewish communalism, which he understood as an attitude
destructive of the deepest traditions of his people. Paul, who had
been a communalist of the first order (a 'Hebrew of the Hebrews'
as he describes himself), was converted precisely out of his
communalism to a universalist standpoint. Henceforth he con-

ceived his entire mission and ministry as the combating and overcoming of the communalism in which he had once been trapped. The significance of Christ, according to Paul, is that he has 'broken down the walls of partition' between communities (Eph. 2.14) so that there can no longer be 'Jew and Gentile' (a cipher for Paul of all fundamental human divisions), but one human community. The complex dialectics of Romans 9 to 11 are concerned with refusing the possibility of ghettoization, refusing to marginalize and exclude those Jews who cannot recognize Jesus as Messiah, with keeping options open. The furious polemics of Galatians are again directed against those who wish to close options, to set limits to community, to exclude those who are not prepared to live according to the law. Paul's vision went beyond racial, national and cultural divisions to embrace class and gender divisions as well. There could be 'no slave or free' in the new humanity, nor even 'male or female'. Writing to a community divided on class lines, and where tensions over the role of women in liturgy were running high, Paul outlined his own vision for the future, his answer to the problem: neither toleration nor fanaticism but the sacramental community.

The sacramental community

Rooted in the sacramentality of community is the community which is sacramental to the nations:

> Thus says God, YHWH . . .
> I am YHWH, I have called you in righteousness, I have taken you by the hand and kept you; I have given you as a covenant to the people, a light to the nations, to open the eyes that are blind, to bring out the prisoners from the dungeon, from the prison those who sit in darkness (Isa. 42.5,6f.).

That Israel exists for the nations is found already in the theology of the Yahwist, in the promise that through Abraham all nations will bless themselves (Gen. 12.3), and this is taken up extensively by Second Isaiah and by later prophets (Isa. 62.2; Zech. 8.23). The existence of Israel for the nations is implied also by the

'Name' theology of Deuteronomy. It is not just the sanctuary but also the people in which God's Name dwells:

> The Lord will establish you as a people holy to himself, as he has sworn to you, if you keep the commandments of the Lord your God and walk in his ways. And all the peoples of the earth shall see that you are called by the name of the Lord; and they shall be afraid of you (Deut. 28.9f.).

The 'they shall be afraid of you' of the last line needs to be glossed by the fourth Servant Song, written at approximately the same time:

> Behold, my servant shall prosper,
> he shall be exalted and lifted up,
> and shall be very high.
> As many were astonished at him –
> his appearance was so marred,
> beyond human semblance,
> and his form beyond that of the sons of men
> so shall he startle many nations;
> kings shall shut their mouths because of him (Isa. 52.13–15).

Deuteronomy was written by a community which felt that the only way to avoid catastrophe was to make the nation a fortified ghetto, where strangers would be welcomed as guests, but otherwise kept at bay. Second Isaiah had a different vision of how the original promise to Abraham might be fulfilled. Whether Jesus consciously looked to this vision or not, the community which he called clearly understood him, and therefore its own mission, in terms of it. For Paul the walls of the ghetto he had striven so hard to keep intact were now levelled: he combed the scriptures for texts which implied the inclusion of the Gentiles in the community (Rom. 15.9f.), and urgently sought to go beyond Asia Minor to Italy and then to Spain (Rom. 15.28) – the whole inhabited earth, the *oikumene*, was included. And this preaching of inclusion, of the end of communalism, was done *necessarily* in weakness, not in power:

God chose what is foolish in the world to shame the wise, God chose what is weak in the world to shame the strong (I Cor. 1.27).

'I was with you,' he says, 'in weakness and in much fear and trembling' (I Cor. 2.3). 'If I must boast, I will boast of the things that show my weakness' (II Cor. 11.30). This is to take the Servant theology of Isaiah and make it both a rule for understanding Christ and for missionary practice. To be a missionary, in Paul's sense *could not be* what it later became, an attempt to enlarge one community at the expense of others. This would be to contradict everything he understood by mission. Those who responded to his preaching of the Messiah crucified in weakness, the *ecclesia,* he understood not as *another* community but as the bearer of the vision of an alternative society, which overcame the divisions, hostilities and destructiveness of human communalism by the weakness of forgiveness, acceptance and love. 'Every one should remain in the state in which he was called', wrote Paul. 'Were you a slave when called? Never mind' (I Cor. 7.20f.).

Does this mean that at heart Paul was an apolitical conformist? Is this good news for slave owners, good news for the rich? Not at all. Paul advocated this policy precisely because he wished to change the whole of society. What good would it do slaves if a few of their number were bought into freedom by a special fund-raising campaign?

Paul's vision was much more radical. Freedom for all in a completely new human community was his horizon. *Ecclesia,* for Paul, was not a unit for the sociologist's attention but, to use Jesus' metaphor, a leaven within the whole universal body politic, changing it from within. This is why, as far as possible, Paul stuck with the synagogue: he was not a sectarian, and sectarianism spelled defeat. The churches he knew were mixed groups – essentially mixed, or the mission had failed: rich and poor, men and women, Jews and Gentiles, which met in peoples' houses to celebrate the resurrection of Jesus and reflect on his life and death but who otherwise got on with their lives. The institutional profile was as low as possible, as a matter of policy: you cannot overcome separation by separating.

Was it already treason when this 'revolutionary cell' model graduated into an institution with authoritarian bishops, as it did in the next century? The move began with the need to combat gnosticism, a radically spiritualizing religious movement which came as near as maybe to swamping the equally radically materialist reform movement which was church in the second century. The choice was, perhaps, between faithfulness to the body and the 'world', in all its Johannine ambiguity, and faithfulness to the church's anti-communal origins. Communalism was already to some extent forced on the church by violent hostility to the new movement on the part of a Judaism which by and large could not accept Jesus as Messiah, and Matthew and John's Gospel reflect these communal pressures. Nevertheless for three centuries, whilst the church was relatively small and sporadically persecuted, compelled therefore to live in the weakness which Paul took as its charter, communalism was kept at bay. Its fate as a communal, and therefore non-alternative, institution was sealed by its elevation to state religion by Constantine, and codified by Justinian in the sixth century. For more than a thousand years it was embraced within the totality of Christendom.

One thing remained: its founding documents, and it is this fact which, against all liberal hostility to the idea, remains the significance of the canon. It is not the case that *panta rei*, as Heraclitus said, that everything is fluid, that everything is dissolved in tradition. When that is the case there is no possibility of fundamental reform. To call scripture 'canon' is to rub the face of the church in the fact that it is only true to itself when it exists in weakness, recognizes its base in the poor, and opposes all forms of communalism. The church has always sought to devise strategies for evading the force of this Word, and some liberal accounts of scripture have to be understood in this way, but its history is one both of evasion, and therefore corruption, but also of those who have heard and attempted to live by the word of judgment at its heart. It is in that sense that the church is, not just theoretically but also in historical practice, *semper reformanda*, always in need of reform.

The base communities of Latin America, the re-discovery of the church of the poor, which is the recovery of the original Pauline charter, are the latest instance of this continual reform. All that the church can offer to the world is an illustration of what it means to live permanently under judgment, what it means to have the gospel of the poor and weak and despised at the heart of a system, to have a rejection of communalism as the first item on your charter. When we talk about the 'inspiration' of scripture it is the existence and continuing power of this word of judgment and reform in the church's life which is at issue, and not an academic discussion about Reformation doctrines or quasi-magical accounts of how God communicates to human beings. The inspiration of scripture is the fact that this collection of documents ticks like a bomb in the hold of the church.

To say that the church is not an ideal community is not just a cynical recognition of the facts. Rather, 'Christianity means community through and in Jesus Christ'.

> By sheer grace God will not permit us to live even for a brief period in a dream world. He does not abandon us to those rapturous experiences and lofty moods that come over us like a dream. God is not a God of emotions but the God of truth.[11]

When we try to live by an ideal, collapse is bound to follow, which is one of the reasons experiments in life together (including marriage) so often end in disillusionment for their participants. An ideal is set up, and when it proves unrealizable the whole, including the gospel which inspired the ideal, is rejected. But 'Christian brotherhood is not an ideal which we must realize; it is rather a reality created by God in Christ in which we may participate'.[12] Bonhoeffer's exposition of this statement takes the form of a contrast of spiritual and human reality, characterized by the opposition of agape and eros, service on the one hand and desire on the other.

In the community of the Spirit the Word of God alone rules; in human community of spirit there rules, along with the Word, the man who is furnished with exceptional powers, experience, and magical suggestive capacities. There God's Word alone is binding; here, besides the Word, men bind others to themselves. There all power, honour and dominion are surrendered to the Holy Spirit; here spheres of power and influence of a personal nature are sought and cultivated.[13]

In the last event, according to Bonhoeffer, human community is based on the idolatry of desire, and is incapable either of putting truth before fellowship, or of loving the enemy. Bonhoeffer's rigorous description of Christian community is all the more impressive in that it is born of the German church struggle, with all its waverings, hesitations and treacheries, as well as its solidarity and faithfulness. It is characterized, however, by the same Lutheran dualism of grace opposed to nature which marks Nygren's book *Agape and Eros*, and this is tilting at windmills. This whole way of posing the problem is a distortion which follows from an inadequate pneumatology which does not sufficiently recognize the work of God in the world apart from the formation of the sacramental community. It may be true that 'Human love can never understand spiritual love', but in that case spiritual love is not restricted to the community under the Word, which is as much marked by the love of desire as every other community.

Human love lives by uncontrolled and uncontrollable dark *desires*; spiritual love lives in the clear light of service ordered by the truth.[14]

Doubtless this is true; but the community marked by spiritual love is as likely to be found in a Gandhian action group or a Marxist cell as in the church, and where it is found, there the Spirit is at work. We cannot deny this for the sake of a dogma.

What is true and important in what Bonhoeffer has to say is that Christian community is in some sense *given* and does not have to be created by our own efforts. It is the fellowship of those who are called, not a club for the like-minded. Moltmann has expressed this by drawing attention to the importance of the two terms 'friend' and 'brother'. Jesus calls his disciples his 'friends' (John 15.14), and to be church is to be the company of the 'friends of Jesus'. The idea of friendship stresses non-necessity and therefore mutual affection and respect: 'Friendship is an open relationship which spreads friendliness, because it combines affection with respect . . . Rightly understood the friend is the person who "loves in freedom".'[15] The advantage of the term 'brother' (or 'sister'!) by contrast is that it emphasizes that fellow members of the community are simply given to us, that we cannot choose them, and that judgment, and therefore reconciliation, begins with the church of God.

That the church is given to us, and that we do not have to create it, needs, however, more exposition. What does it mean for those situations where both oppressed and oppressor are to be found within the church? What can it mean to talk of 'community' when not only is the suffering of one *not* the suffering of others, but the suffering of some is the *precondition for the well-being of others*?[16] Is it not more accurate to speak of a community of interest (and to that extent of the like-minded) – between, for instance, those who struggle for justice, no matter what their religious beliefs, than of a community which embraces those committed to mutually antagonistic views of the world, views understood on both sides to be de-humanizing and therefore, to use Boff's term, 'non-Christic'? Why devote energy needed to work for change in the world to trying to accomplish change in the church, when the experience of 'church' makes the struggle for humanization more difficult than ever? Are not religious communities *necessarily* communal so long as they hold together people whose interests are opposed and keep apart people whose interests are the same? Given that the church embraces people of irreconcilably opposed views throughout the world, what does it mean to continue using the language of 'brother and sister', and what does it mean for the church to be the sacramental community? Two responses may be suggested.

The community we call 'church' is not primarily an institution but something which is continually coming into being, an event within the reading of the Word and the celebration of the eucharist ('where the Word is preached and the sacraments rightly administered'), and the personal, political and social practice which follows from this. Although the being of the church is not in the least exhausted by these activities, they are nevertheless the core activities which constitute it and give it identity. To be 'in Christ' means to be given one's identity within this pattern of activity, along with the rest of the community which reads, hears and celebrates. That the church is given us means that who we are is constituted by the telling of the Christian story, that 'my' story is *this* story. The story concerns betrayal, torture, death, forgiveness.

The whole story of Jesus, in a way, is an exemplification of what it means to love our enemy, namely to refuse to let go of his or her humanity. It is not the community of 'peace at any price', of a papering over of divisions, of a worthless reconciliation. Such a reconciliation would not have brought Jesus to the cross. But if the poor, say the members of the Latin American base communities, stay in the same church as their killers and torturers it is because, receiving their identity from Jesus, they refuse to let go of their enemies' humanity. To stay in the same church as your oppressor is to refuse to allow victory to the oppressor's vision both of the human condition and of the church. It is to say that at bottom to be human is not to be a wolf; to refuse to allow the church, the bearer of Jesus' story, to be co-opted and monopolized by the believers in cynical 'realism'. None of this is to preclude the most strenuous opposition to oppression within the church. Living by forgiveness and love does not mean being supine, which Jesus never was. The church is in its essence a resistance movement to the forces of 'death', and therefore resistance must be expected from its members. But resistance to oppression begins precisely with resistance to the enemy's self-definition.

The oppressor, like Nietzsche's 'super man', puts himself beyond the standards of good and evil. Refusing to allow him to do that is what it means practically to forgive, to hang on to his humanity. As the discussion of the incarnation made clear, human being is not constituted by an incorruptible core, but is constituted by relations. As a child reared by animals does not grow to be a human being, so we can opt out of the human condition, we can renounce our humanness, we can choose the void of torture and extermination. The power of the poor in history, the power of forgiveness, is to refuse to accept this option, to hold on to the torturer as he seeks to hurl himself into hell, the destruction of his human being. Precisely this is how Stephen understood the force of Jesus' example (Acts 7.60).

Secondly, Paul opposed the sacramental community to the destructiveness of communalism not as an ideal group or a model for every other community to follow but simply as the community which always lives under judgment, and therefore exists continually *in the process of reform*. What sparks this perpetual reformation is the vision of community which arose from the life and teaching of Jesus and which he spelled out to the class-ridden society of Corinth:

vision as judgment

> Now there are varieties of gifts, but the same Spirit; and there are varieties of service, but the same Lord; and there are varieties of working, but it is the same God who inspires them all in every one. To each is given the manifestation of the Spirit for the common good (I Cor. 12.4–7).

The sacramental community bears the vision of community as sacramental, of a community where human difference, of age, race, sex and ability is not simply acknowledged but *celebrated* as a manifestation of the infinite variety of God's Spirit. Variety does not mean contest or rivalry, because the rootedness of all gifts in the one Spirit is recognized:

> For by one Spirit we were all baptized into one body – Jews or Greeks, slaves or free – and all were made to drink of one Spirit (I Cor. 12.13).

In the light of Jesus' crucifixion and resurrection Paul was unable to read history in the old way, but acquired a more universal perspective. All human history was now subsumed first under Adam and then under Christ. In the new humanity differences did not cease, but they ceased to be fundamental. What was important was being part of one 'body'. In the body, corresponding to what he had learned from 'Messiah Jesus', who took the form of a slave, 'those parts of the body which we think less honourable we invest with greater honour':

> God has so composed the body, giving the greater honour to the inferior part, that there may be no discord in the body, but that the members may have the same care for one another. If one member suffers, all suffer together; if one member is honoured, all rejoice together (I Cor. 12.24–26).

This is not, as it is often taken to be, a blueprint for the church, but a blueprint for a new humanity. The new society is characterized by giving priority to the weak, and learning to live by mutual caring. As we have sought to emasculate scripture, so all sorts of ploys have been adopted to rob this vision of its power: it has been said to apply only to the church, and then only to specific groups within the church such as monastic houses. It has been dismissed as an 'interim ethic', only conceivable when it was believed that the end of the world was directly at hand. It is regularly dismissed as 'unrealistic' because it fails to take account of the human need for 'incentive'. These responses are to be expected, and it is to be expected that they dress themselves in religious garb, but they should be recognized for what they are: the crude fabrications of the ideology of greed and power. The church is sacramental as, and only as, it continues to live by this vision, continues to confront the 'unbelieving' world with it (which is the meaning of 'mission'), and continues to try and reform itself according to it. Living and prophesying by this vision is what discernment means for the life of the church.

6

Spirit in the Flesh

Agape versus eros

The publication, in 1930, of the first volume of Anders Nygren's great study *Agape and Eros*, set the terms for the discussion of the Christian doctrine of love for the rest of the century. Nygren argued for a fundamental antagonism between two kinds of love, eros being the upward seeking for fulfilment through the beautiful, agape being the downward outpouring of love for the unlovable and unlike. The one originated with Greek thought, and found classic expression in Plato; the other found supreme expression in the New Testament. They represented, he said, 'two opposite attitudes to life' and were by nature 'completely antithetic'. Here he could count on the support of the most distinguished Plato scholar of the day, Wilamowitz-Möllendorff, who emphatically repudiated the idea that Platonic eros coincided in any way with Christian agape. If Plato and Paul could have met, he said, they would have made nothing of each other. In his account of eros Nygren gave scant attention to what he called 'vulgar eros', sexuality. He is at pains to emphasize that he is talking about something entirely 'spiritual', even though it begins with an experience of the beautiful. Eros may be kindled by sensible beauty, but its function is to ascend to the supra-sensible beauty of the world of Forms. Agape, on the other hand, 'is the direct opposite of that love which is called out by the worthiness of its object and so may be said to be a recognition of the value and attractiveness of its object. The man whom God loves has not any value in himself. His value consists simply in the fact that God loves him.'[1] Agape is a 'theocentric' concept, essentially the divine forgiveness of human beings, whilst eros is anthropocentric and egocentric. Eros postulates a fundamental kinship with the Divine, which from the standpoint of agape is presumption and a failure to recognize the impassable gulf between God and man.

Nygren has to concede, however, that even in the New Testament, in the Johannine writings, there is a 'weakening down' of the idea of agape which prepares the ground for that later confusion of the two kinds of love which received classic expression in Augustine, who fused agape and eros in the concept of *Caritas*. For Augustine, *all* love was 'acquisitive love'.

> To love means to direct one's longing and desire to an object by the possession of which one expects to be made happy. The idea of love as desire and its connection with the search for happiness betray Augustine's original Eros-attitude and the eudaemonism of the philosophy of late antiquity.[2]

Augustine replaced the original stark opposition of agape and eros with a quite different, and much less fundamental, opposition of *caritas* and *cupiditas*. Here the *nature* of love is the same in both cases, because both seek their own *bonum* but *cupiditas* mistakes its object, fixing on created, transitory things, whilst *caritas* seeks its rest in God. *Caritas* enjoys God and uses the world whilst *cupiditas* enjoys the world and uses God. Augustine identifies the ascending love he learned from Neoplatonism with the love of the First Commandment, but what this means, according to Nygren, is that even though God is described as the *highest* good, he is in fact degraded to the level of a means for the satisfaction of human desire.[3]

This synthesis effected by Augustine, powerfully reinforced by the pure eros religion of Dionysius the Areopagite, determined the *caritas* theology of the Middle Ages, of which not only Aquinas but also Dante was an outstanding representative. It was Luther, according to Nygren, who tore up this synthesis, and went back to the pure New Testament concept of agape. For Nygren, revelation as we have defined it could *only* happen through agape and *never* through eros. Eros could only be redeemed insofar as it was sublimated into agape. He maintained that 'sensual love has no place in a discussion of love in the religious sense, whether in the context of the Eros or of the Agape motif'.[4] The only place where it was taken up, as far as he was concerned, was in the Gnostic orgies of the second century, the lowest form of all eros religion. In this hostility at least Nygren has something in common with Augustine. Discussing marriage Augustine could write that whilst it was honourable,

> yet, whenever it comes to the actual process of generation, the very embrace which is lawful and honourable cannot be effected without the ardour of lust . . . (which) whether following or preceding the will, does somehow, by a power of its own, move the members which cannot be moved simply by the will, and in this manner it shows itself not to be the servant of a will which commands it, but rather to be the punishment of a will which disobeys it . . . This is the carnal concupiscence which, while it is no longer accounted sin in the regenerate yet in no case happens to nature except from sin.[5]

This opinion of Augustine, not the strongest of his words on sexuality, can be found echoed by most great Christian teachers up to the present century. As Suzanne Lilar puts it, Christianity both despised the flesh and cultivated an obsession with it. Instead of a sacred doctrine of love, as there was in the popular Greek tradition, or a philosophy of love, as there was in Plato, 'there was now a casuistry'. No amount of preaching could rob eros of its power, but what it could do was to produce guilt at its effects. This negative attitude to sexuality is not entirely without grounds. In the tradition which gave Christians their world, scripture, there seemed to be a *prima facie* case for a real opposition of spirit and flesh, and there was a profound suspicion, emanating from the Greek tradition, and vividly

This is when H. of B is able to manoeuvre because she talks about image/flesh + likeness/reason

illustrated in the quotation from Augustine, of anything which was not consciously *willed*. Subordination to the merely instinctual seemed to place human beings once again on the level of the animals. It was above all in rationality, and the ability to use reason for ethical purposes, that human beings could be said to possess God's image and stand 'little lower than the angels'. Furthermore, human experience in this area is, after all, highly ambiguous: no human society has yet structured relationships between the sexes in such a way that one sex does not dominate the other. And there is the fact that, as Rosemary Haughton has put it, amongst human experiences Romantic passion is peculiarly open to corruption. 'There is something so extremely nasty about what happens to Romantic passion when it "goes wrong",' she writes, 'that it is not very surprising that Romance itself had generally been viewed with suspicion by both Church and State, and indeed by "all sensible people".'[6]

Nevertheless there are compelling grounds from within both the origin and the development of the Christian tradition for seeking to 'discern the Spirit' in the experience of sexual love, so long as we bear in mind the warning of Charles Williams. 'It will be an unfortunate day for Romantic Theology,' he wrote, 'if it ever gets into the hands of official ministers of the Church . . . The covenanted mercies are their concern. This, uncovenanted, rides in our very nature – within and without the Church; say, rather, this is that ancient covenant which reveals what all the others support: "My covenant shall be in your flesh."'[7]

Spirit and flesh

'Those who live according to the flesh,' says Paul, 'set their minds on things of the flesh, but those who live according to the Spirit set their minds on the things of the Spirit. To set the mind on the flesh is death, but to set the mind on the Spirit is life and peace. For the mind that is set on the flesh is hostile to God; it does not submit to God's law, indeed it cannot; and those who are in the flesh cannot please God' (Rom. 8.5–8). It is of course clear that 'flesh' cannot simply be identified *tout court* with sensuality. Exegetes usually characterize the 'outlook of the flesh' as, rather, the attempt to live without God, 'trust in oneself as being able to procure life through one's own strength and accomplishment', as Bultmann puts it. Thus Paul's question, 'Having begun with the Spirit are you now ending with the flesh?' (Gal. 3.3) clearly refers to reliance on the law rather than on grace, and the same applies to the discussion in Phillipians (Phil. 3.3–7).

Nevertheless, we have to beware of trimming scripture to fit our own world-view, now overtly in favour of sexual freedom. We have to beware, in other words, of being as securely trapped in our totality on this issue as, for instance, Harnack was in his political theology. When Paul lists the 'sins of the flesh' he names 'fornication, impurity, licentiousness, idolatry, sorcery, enmity, strife, jealousy, anger, selfishness, dissension, party spirit, envy, drunkenness, carousing and the like' (Gal. 5.19–21). The identification of sexuality with sin, strongly evidenced in the tradition and reinforced by the privatization of religion after the industrial revolution, is quite easily taken from this list, an identification aided by what appears to be Paul's lukewarm attitude to marriage in I Corinthians 7. Bertrand Russell wrote that Paul spoke of marriage like the doctor he saw for advice on giving up smoking: when tempted, his doctor said, suck an acid drop. Paul regarded marriage in the same way: not as much fun as fornication, but better for you.[8] But Paul begins his list of sins of the flesh with sexuality not because, like Augustine, he is neurotic about it, but because of his conviction that the body is the temple of the Spirit:

> Shun fornification (*porneia*). Every other sin which a man commits is outside the body; but the fornicator sins against his own body. Do you not know that your body is a temple of the Holy Spirit within you, which you have from God? (I Cor. 6.18f.).

Paul, in other words, is refusing to make concessions to a dualism of flesh and spirit; he is acknowledging that in some way the physical *is* the spiritual. This fact, implicit in the beliefs at the very core of the Christian faith – belief in the incarnation and resurrection of the body – both grounds a belief in the sanctity of sexual relations, the claim that we encounter *God* in them, and gives rise to the neurotic obsession with sex as the archetypal sin in Christian tradition. It is this unhealthy obsession which accounts for the various heretical movements such as the 'Brethren of the Free Spirit' in the Middle Ages, or the Ranters in the seventeenth century, which all sought salvation through abandoning sexual restraint. The Ranter Lawrence Clarkson wrote that 'till you can lie with all women as one woman and not judge it sin you can do nothing but sin', and some of the medieval protagonists attributed a transcendental mystical value to the sexual act itself. Between these two extremes, the ascetic and the way of excess, there has been a *via affirmativa*, the approach to God through images, rooted, perhaps, in the inclusion of the Song of Songs in the canon (where the love of the man and woman was translated by agape in the Septuagint!), and for which the classical figure is Dante. It is to Dante and his commentators – especially, in more recent times, Charles Williams – that we look for an understanding of Spirit in the flesh.

Revelation through eros?

Running counter to the main stream of thought on agape and eros we may discern a narrow alternative tradition which can be traced through Heloise, the Courtly love tradition, Dante, John Donne, and Blake to the 'theologians of Romantic love', Coventry Patmore, Charles Williams and, more recently, Rosemary Haughton. Within the tradition of reflection systematized by Williams and Haughton there is an attempt to understand sexual experience theologically above all by appealing to the theology of the Trinity, Incarnation and the sacraments. Coventry Patmore speaks for this tradition in appealing to the significance of God's being as Trinity. Man is made in God's image, said Patmore, and God is '"an Act", the Act of primary Love, the "embrace" as the Church styles it, of the First and Second Persons, that embrace being the proceeding Spirit of universal Life.'[9]

In this appeal to the Trinity Patmore anticipates the twentieth-century discussion of God's being as Act and, properly, seeks to understand that Act of Love. When we speak of the Trinity we mean the 'embrace' of the First and Second Persons and their unity in the Spirit of Life which proceeds from that embrace. All the loves we know are 'more or less remote echoes and refrains' of this being-in-Act. 'This "dry doctrine" of the Trinity, or primary Act of Love,' Patmore wrote, 'is the keystone of all living knowledge and delight. God himself becomes a concrete object and an intelligible joy when contemplated as the eternal felicity of a lover with the Beloved.'

In making this appeal Patmore draws our attention to a weakness in Nygren's whole discussion. Nygren rejects Augustine's trinitarian theology, which takes human self-love as the primary analogue for understanding God's reality but is unable to offer a *trinitarian* account of the being of God as love in terms of agape. Contemporary discussion, by contrast, has wanted to insist that the doctrine of the Trinity shows us relationships as in some sense at the heart of reality. If it is true that the need implicit in eros makes this unsuitable as an image of the divine love, nevertheless the concept of agape needs to be extended, somewhat as Augustine extended it, to take into account the love of the three Persons of the Godhead *in itself*, which cannot be described as love for the unworthy and unlike. Nygren's critique of Augustine may be wide of the mark because Augustine was not so much misled by Neo-Platonism into combining agape and eros, as led to do so by the necessities of trinitarian reflection. Such reflection requires us to think of the reciprocity we have traditionally associated with eros *in God*. Precisely this affirmation has been stated most impressively by Haughton:

The passion of love which offered itself to the point at which estranged human kind could receive the torrent of divine *amour voulu* is the demonstration of the inmost reality of the Three in One. It is the point at which we are enabled to see, in direct and unambiguous human terms, the nature of that which is the very being of God. The love which incarnate

Wisdom so longs to give back to its Source and Origin in one
unbroken movement of ecstatic joy and thanksgiving, and
that joy, that intensity of exchange of Being is the one called
Spirit. That which the Father breathes, speaks, expends is his
own being, and it only *is* in being given. Therefore also it only
is in being received, and the essence of that exchanged being
(Exchange itself) is the one who from the generative embrace
between Holiness and Wisdom has being as life, gives life and
praises life.[10]

An appeal to the love which is Trinity is, then, a common
theme in the development of Romantic Theology. Paul Avis
has also pointed out that if we deny eros in God, then eros in
human beings has no source, analogy or hope of redemption in
God, and our erotic nature, as such, alienates us from God.[11]
But this would entail Manichaean doubts about the goodness
of creation, about whether the creation was wholly the product
of God, and therefore about whether human beings exist in
God's image. This is too high a price to pay for the proper
caution against identifying the holy and creative love of God
with naked libido, or the power of fertility *per se*.

A second theme of what Williams called 'Romantic Theology' was the significance of the Incarnation. According to Patmore the denial of the sanctity of erotic love meant that 'the
doctrine of the Incarnation has been emasculated and deprived
of its inmost significance and power'. He believed, however,
that we were witnessing a profound transformation when 'the
"one mortal thing of worth immortal" is about to be enthron-
ed in Catholic psychology as it never was before'.[12] Patmore
wants to say that the doctrine that God took flesh confers
sanctity on the flesh itself and that, therefore, human sexual
love might properly be a sacrament of God's own affirmation
of flesh.

This theme was taken up in a most remarkable way by
Charles Williams in his early, and still unpublished, essay
'Outlines of Romantic Theology', which he wrote in 1924. 'The
principles of Romantic Theology,' he wrote, 'can be reduced to a

single formula: which is, the identification of love with Jesus Christ, and of marriage with his life.'

> Every Mass was said once on Calvary, and we do not so much repeat as are in the Mass absorbed into that eternal offering. So each marriage was lived in His life, though – in terms of time – it waits its due time in the order of the universe to become manifest . . . (The business of true lovers) is not to be, but to know that they are, His symbols, and that their marriage is His life.[13]

As Rosemary Haughton puts it, the experience of Romantic passion offers us not only an *analogy* of human divine relationships but an *example* of it. Experience becomes the vehicle of transcendence, and revelation occurs. In Iris Murdoch's novel *The Sacred and Profane Love Machine*, one of the characters reflects on his adulterous love:

> Sin was an awful private happiness blotting out all else; only it was not sin, it was glory . . . blazing with light and as large as the universe. Everything he had done before seemed feeble, shadowy and insincere. A combination of pure free creation and pure causality now felicitously ruled his life . . . This was not just intense sexual bliss, it was absolute metaphysical justification. The world in its detail was revealed at last to an indubitable insight. His whole being was engaged, he was identified with his real self, he fully inhabited his own nature for the first time in his life.[14]

Iris Murdoch here gives fine expression to one of the most common as well as one of the most important of human experiences and illustrates how it comes with the force of revelation. Put theologically, this vision is about Spirit in the flesh. In the vision of the romantic poets it was a love which sprang into being precisely through seeing and responding to the physical presence and beauty of the beloved. Rosemary Haughton argues that it was only Christianity, rooted in the flesh-taking, which could create the cultural environment in which such a concept could take root and flourish. Only Christian doctrine teaches that the divine can be not merely immanent in or symbolized by material bodies but actually enfleshed, and only this doctrine could make such an articulation of experience permissible and therefore possible.[15] Williams expounded this theme, in his early essay, through the unlikely means of an exegesis of the central texts of the Book of Common Prayer. Every marriage, he argues, can be assumed into Christ's life – his conception, birth, temptations, failures, death and resurrection. What this means, for instance for the birth of Christ, is that the birth of love in us is a kind of immaculate conception. The Beloved appears to the lover

> archetypal, the alpha and omega of creation; without father or mother, without human ties of any sort, for she is before humanity, the first created of God. To her, for example, may be decently applied all the titles of the Litany of Loretto . . . She is the Mother of Love, purissima, inviolata, admirabilis . . . Mater Salvatoris.[16]

Analysing the theology of courtly love Haughton believes that what the (male) lover encounters in the beloved is divine Wisdom, 'the radiance of the eternal God, and he sees her in the very *flesh* of the beloved'.[17] In this way Haughton too, along with Charles Williams, claims that a human being, precisely in his or her fleshliness, may be God-bearer, Christ and Saviour.

In the fourth chapter of 'Outlines' Williams turned to the Communion Service and quoted Patmore: 'The Blessed Sacrament is first of all a symbol of the beloved; afterwards the beloved is a symbol of the Blessed Sacrament.' Every moment of the Holy Communion Service of 1662 is glossed, with sexual love in mind. The reception of communion has its analogue in sexual intercourse. In intercourse, he believes, 'the presence of Love, that is of Christ, is sacramentally imparted by each to the other'. Unless this were so, 'it is difficult to see in what way marriage itself is more sacramental than any other occupation'. In the love of the marriage night 'the devout and Catholic lover bestows and receives . . . the Real Presence of the Most Sacred Body and Blood'.[18]

As one reads both Patmore and Williams on this theme the question constantly arises whether the boundaries of blasphemy and idolatry have not been overstepped. It was not simple prudishness, nor the church's neurosis about sex, which gave the ecclesiastical censors problems with the *Divina Commedia* where Beatrice appears as a mediator of Dante's salvation. It is a much more fundamental question of identifying the means of grace and understanding what we can say about them when we have done that. 'There has been and is, now as always, only one question about this state of things,' wrote Williams, 'is it serious? is it capable of intellectual treatment? is it capable of belief, labour, fruition? is it (in some sense or other) true?'[19] There is no doubt that Williams' bold speculations are a long way removed from the theology of the Christian scriptures, even that of the Song of Songs, though this allegation was for a very long time levelled at trinitarian doctrine. But the decisive question of discernment is, for Williams, precisely displacement. Commenting on the second commandment, the proscription of images (for the whole Decalogue was read in the 1662 rite) he wrote

> It is not so much to intellectual ideas that this refers, as to a state of soul which rests upon some self-created phantasy and does not lay itself wholly open to the Otherness from himself, the not-himselfness, of the approaching Power, divine or human.[20]

Revelation is what we cannot tell ourselves. It is as revelation occurs in the encounter of love, as we learn the truth about ourselves and the world because we are taken outside of ourselves through the Other, that we can speak of the Spirit. Sexual love may be an experience of the divine as it breaks us open, takes us out of our totality, teaches us vulnerability and generosity of spirit. The other, we have established, is the primary sacrament of God – the one who is other to the whole of creation. In the political and community context this is the other as poor, the other who stands outside my economic totality, the other in whom I have to see God in political process. In sexual love it is the other as the sacrament of God's joy, beauty and self-giving, the other as the sacrament of celebration which lies on the far side of revolution. All sacraments are in different ways eschatological, and here we celebrate God's glory, for 'the glory of God is a living human being', as Irenaeus said. If we do not meet God here, where we give ourselves most deeply, most wholly and totally, then were do we meet him? The entire work of Dante, says Williams, unwittingly echoing the trinitarian formula of Karl Barth, 'is a description of the great act of knowledge, in which Dante himself is the Knower, and God is the Known, and Beatrice is the Knowing'.[21]

Underlying this seemingly extravagant description is a theology of grace, the exposition of what it means to say that the Holy Spirit meets us and moves us from within, of what it means concretely that it is 'not I, but Christ in me', 'not we who pray, but the Spirit praying through us'. If we claim that God can be encountered in the deepest experiences of sexual love, this is on the grounds of the creative and redemptive aspects of this experience. If 'lust' is the name for sexual experience which is purely about self-gratification, without real concern for or involvement with the other, and therefore about idolatry, making our own satisfaction absolute, then by the same token in the deepest forms of sexual encounter there is a holiness, that is a purity and depth of recognition of the other, which speaks of the presence of the holy God.

Robin Zaehner maintained that what was blasphemous was not the comparison of the sexual act to mystical union with God but rather any attempt to degrade that act in which human beings resemble God in their self-giving and ability to create.[22] God is encountered in and through the other, when their strangeness, otherness and beauty is respected, reverenced and celebrated precisely as praise of the Creator. In such experiences God gives himself as Knower, Known, and Knowing, as Revealer, Revelation and Revealedness, and is interior to every moment of the event of revelation. We are encountered by him at every stage. It is such a theology of grace, rooted, as Williams said, in the flesh-taking, and in the existence of God as relation, in the infinite variety of God's presence, which grounds sacramental thinking, and which legitimates talk of the experience not of any spirit but of the Holy Spirit, in the flesh.

It should be noted that this is the exact opposite of Jung's assertion that the divine can be encountered in sexuality. For him the Divine is a transcendent force which 'obliterates and consumes everything individual'.[23] I maintain, to the contrary, that experience of the divine is to be had in experience of the irreducibility, and of the graciousness, the grace-bearing character, of the other.

The corruption of eros

Marriage is a sacrament, and sacraments are patterns of graciousness, areas of 'holy ground' in human experience, which involve in a central way the affirmation of the material and the bodily. This affirmation brings with it at the same time a demand for truthfulness in what we do in the body, a conformity to actual bodily facts as expressions of real personal meeting. This demand, says Rosemary Haughton,

> makes us perceive as untruthful any use of bodies (that is, of people) as sexual which fails to express at every level of the human person the full symbolism of bodily and sexual being, which is to be exchanged physically and emotionally and in relation to history and to the community, and as particular and passionate incarnation of divine love, totally given and received, creatively poured out without reserve and in eternal fidelity. That is the kind of thing sexuality is and says, in itself. That is why the conscious commitment to such an exchange has to have the character of 'sacrament', for it makes actual and bodily in a special and particular way the passionate love of Christ, which gives life.[24]

A sacrament is a created reality through which the Spirit of God gifts himself to us. If the relationship in which we come closest to another person, bind ourselves to them for life, and discover the spiritual in and through the physical is not this, then what is? But just because this experience is so immediate and so

total, and because it involves the gratification of our deepest
desires, it is also here that we run the greatest danger of deception
and idolatry. The religion of the 'natural man' has always been a
deification of the powers of sex and fertility, which always
involves yet another form of 'betting on the strong', on the gifted
and beautiful. In its contemporary manifestation it is marked by
the hedonism and consumerism symbolized most effectively by
the 'soft' pornography market. The assumption of this market is
that a beautiful woman is basically a plaything for a man, and
exists along with his large house and powerful car to underline his
own importance and power. Sexuality becomes a commodity like
everything else. The struggle to the death waged by the prophets
of Israel against the priests of Baal and Astarte was a struggle
against a religion which sanctified power as such and champion-
ed the strong and the beautiful against the weak. Capitalism
worships the same deities in only slightly more sophisticated
guise.

Furthermore, the 'Yes' which we have to say to sexuality
cannot be unqualified for two reasons. First there is, as Rosemary
Haughton remarks, the particularly hideous way in which this
experience goes wrong, documented more or less daily in our
newspapers. Susanne Heine records how, in April 1986, Raphael,
aged 3, died in Vienna after being maltreated by his mother's boyfriend. Mother and boyfriend were copulating alongside the child
as he was dying. It was said to have been an overwhelming erotic
experience. Suzanne Lilar records a similar horrific story.[25] The
logic of pornography, which is sex where power replaces love, is
death, a fact copiously illustrated both in fact and fiction. Torture
of political opponents and the destruction of a woman for sexual
pleasure are obviously related. Both are about the absolutization
of power which, since it cannot be a power to create *ex nihilo*, has
to be about the power to destroy. All forms of lust are forms of
indulgence of the self which ignore the other, and sexual lust is
related, as we see from de Sade, with the lust to destroy, to
desecrate the image, to annihilate and render inhuman anything
which threatens the absoluteness of my ego.

Less dreadful and more common, if not indeed universal, is the experience of self-deception through infatuation, a theme so wittily parodied in Shakespeare's *A Midsummer Night's Dream*: 'Methought I was enamoured of an ass!' If the Spirit of God can encounter us in sexual encounter, equally not every chance infatuation is the work of the Spirit of God. To counter self-deception the entire Jewish and Christian tradition places sexuality within the framework of a covenant – a permanent commitment between two people which can be broken only by death – and this covenant is given to be offered up to and taken into the embracing love of God. The covenant of love between two people which we call marriage echoes God's own commitment to his people, to the church and to creation, a commitment which is irrevocable. The point of the analogy between husband and wife and Christ and the church is precisely the framework of absolute mutual commitment. Certainly such a covenant is intended to include life together and the possibility of bringing up children within the relation of a continuing and exploratory love, and this explains the church's proper refusal to admit divorce as a norm. But a number of questions crowd in here. If divorce cannot be admitted as a norm, can the church re-marry divorcees? How are we to understand other relationships of depth and commitment which supervene on marriage, which may or may not be actually adulterous? And, if we affirm that God meets us in sexual encounter, where does this leave the traditional Christian emphasis on celibacy?

The question of remarriage after divorce is, surely, the question of whether resurrection may be experienced in this life, which I have already answered in the affirmative. Divorce may represent a cheap way out of resolvable differences. It may involve refusal to live by the command to forgive the other 'until seventy times seven' and in turn to be forgiven. There are, on the other hand, certainly cases where it is the only human option and where the demands of love require it. If that is the case, what should be our attitude to remarriage in church? Decisive in answering this question is the fact that in any marriage it is the partners who perform the sacramental act, by making the covenant with one another. They then come to the church to 'share their joy', as the

Anglican *Alternative Service Book* puts it, and to ask for their
covenant to be blessed. If this is the case, then the distinction
between a 'marriage proper' and the blessing of marriage which
the church permits after divorce seems casuistry, and it is
difficult to imagine Christ countenancing it.

That we may 'fall in love' not once but several times is, for
good or ill, one of the commonest human experiences, and we
have to respond to it theologically. The absolute prohibition of
adultery in the Old Testament, which incurred stoning to death,
sprang from a view of woman as part of the man's property,
reflected in differing penalties for men and women. The real
issue in adultery, as we would view it today, is betrayal of trust
and commitment, and this clearly involves a quite different
response. What are we to do with the experience of 'falling in
love' which always comes to us as a 'given' and with the power
of revelation? To reject it as satanic temptation all seem to those
involved like the sin against the Holy Spirit, calling that which is
good evil; yet no more than divorce can it be recommended as a
norm. The significance of the fact that we encounter *God* in the
sexual is that the depth involved implies monogamy and the
need for a lifetime's commitment to fathom that depth. And yet
writing out of his own highly ambiguous experience Karl Barth
could say:

> Let it not be forgotten, there is genuine, strong and whole
> hearted love even in relations which cannot flower in regular
> marriage, but which in all their fragmentariness are not mere
> sin and shame, and do not wholly lack the character of
> marriage. Furthermore, in this sphere especially there is to be
> noted a certain zealously practised restraint against the desire
> or preference for strange fruit.[26]

Here, as in all cases, the freedom of God's rule transcends what
we rightly understand on the basis of the revelation in scripture
to be the norm. That, again, is not *carte blanche* for every
conceivable type of irregular relationship. But that God can be
encountered in such covenants cannot be doubted.

For nineteen hundred years the church treated celibacy as a 'counsel of perfection'. In doing so it was appealing to an explicitly dualist anthropology which thought of the body warring against the soul, and believed that the denial of the body was the supreme weapon in the Christian's armoury. Today a non-dualist anthropology, which emphasizes Spirit in the flesh, is in danger of so emphasizing the importance of the sexual as to imply that there are no real relationships, no wholeness, without it. At this point we must be careful not to stress the doctrine of the Incarnation so much that we lose sight of the historical Jesus. We say that Jesus was 'the proper Man', but Jesus himself was celibate. We are not tempted to deny the depth of his relationships with Martha or Mary Magdalen because they were not overtly sexual. The contemporary commonplace that all our relationships are sexual is, after all, merely a half truth. 'Sexual' does not mean genital, and to take genital sexuality as a paradigm for all other forms of relationship would be intolerably impoverishing. It is not as if it is *only* here that we reach the deepest depths of the other. It has been suggested that religious celibacy might be a sign that all our relationships are ultimately rooted in God.[27] Of course it is the argument of this book that God is encountered precisely in and through political, community and personal encounter, and yet all these relationships are *sacramental*, they point away from themselves to God. With the older tradition, then, we have to continue to affirm that God may be encountered in all forms of loving relationship. The need to highlight sexual relationships in particular follows partly from what our faith has to tell us about flesh, and God in the flesh, and partly from the consistent flight from this insight until the present century. We need to move now from an opposition of agape and eros to an understanding of their dialectical relationship.

The dialectic of agape and eros

Scorning the thesis of Denis de Rougemont (accepted, amongst others, by C. S. Lewis and Rosemary Haughton) that Romantic love is an invention of twelfth-century Europe, Suzanne Lilar sees it, more convincingly, as an essential and unavoidable part of being human. Put theologically, her demand to recognize God at work in the erotic would be grounded neither in God's being as triune, nor in the Incarnation, but in the facts of our created reality, especially in the androgynous aspects of our biological make-up. She accepts Nygren's account of the antipathy of the Gospels to erotic love but wishes to insist that eros can be a mediator from the flesh to the spirit. The function of erotic love, she says, is to 'dig out and develop the least germ of spirit', and the art of love is 'a long elucidation of the spirit'.[28] Iris Murdoch again illustrates this contention:

> Intense mutual erotic love, love which involves with the flesh all the most refined sexual being of the spirit, which reveals and perhaps even *ex nihilo* creates spirit as sex . . . presents itself as such a dizzily lofty value that even to speak of 'enjoying' it seems a sacrilege. It is something to be undergone upon one's knees. And where it exists it cannot but shed a blazing light of justification upon its own scene, a light which can leave the rest of the world dark indeed.[29]

Far from belonging to the realm of 'dark desires', eros is essentially lucid, accompanied by light, and love is essentially noetic, as Plato taught: 'If it is true that "the Spirit feels nothing except with the help of the body", it is also true that the body is called upon, is appointed to bring the spirit into the world, to be *delivered* of it.'[30] Erotic love is not in need of being hallowed by a sacrament because it is itself *sacral*: able to communicate the sacred, by which Lilar means 'absolute otherness, ambiguity, ambivalence, polarity, the twofold character of positivity and negativity'. As a characterization of the sacred these descriptions, with the exception of the first, smack far more of Gnostic 'mysteries' than of the holiness of the God of whom the Christian scriptures speak. Lilar is right, however, that the division of love into sacred and profane is disastrous and leads to the substitution of 'magic for the sacred, the marvellous for the religious'. If nothing else, the loss of depth in contemporary Western experiences of erotic love cries out for a fresh theological

But this is the male problem: God = freedom — & can't be free unless separate from influence

appraisal, a fresh understanding of where *God* is in this experience.

It is instructive to compare Lilar's account of the sacred with Nygren's account of agape. He characterizes agape as being in the first place spontaneous and 'uncaused' – unrelated to the worthiness of the object. It is this love in itself which bestows value on its object, and it is this alone which opens the way of fellowship with God. Eros always contains an element of self-love; for this, agape has no place. But are these aspects of agape in fact not found in erotic love? Such love is spontaneous and 'uncaused' in the sense that it is 'for nothing', even if it recognizes beauty and glory in the Beloved, a beauty and glory which others, notoriously, may be quite unable to see. And eros, too, is capable of an extraordinary degree of self-sacrifice.

Along these lines the Austrian theologian Susanne Heine has argued that we should think in terms neither of the confusion of agape and eros, nor of their absolute opposition, but rather of the recognition of a dialectical tension between them. She accepts the broad outlines of Nygren's characterization of the differences between the two types of love, and draws attention especially to the violence inherent in what he called 'vulgar Eros', a violence which underlines the necessity of making a distinction. Nevertheless the way forward is not through a repudiation of eros in favour solely of agape, for agape too can be destructive. Agape can rob people of their vitality: 'Eros can tear people apart . . . agape can throttle people, make them lose their nerve.'[31] And eros cannot in fact be overcome. Denied, it goes underground, and emerges even more destructive: 'human eros may not be killed off.' Therefore a dialectic is called for:

> Dialectic means that the one, eros, not only conflicts with the other, agape, so that each limits the other, but that the one is transcended in the other and that therefore the two cannot get on without each other.[32]

Ironically, in view of Nygren's use of Luther to support his position, Heine appeals to Luther as the protagonist of a genuine 'eros theology'. According to her, Luther's is an 'erotic' theology to the degree that it does not deny the experience of eros, either human eros in all its ambivalence, or the eros of God who elects and rejects, comes near and remains alien. But here human eros is neither divinized nor diabolized, and the dialectic of love retains its tension.[33]

Her account of the relation of eros and agape echoes Nygren's but goes beyond it. On the one hand there is a real distinction, which must be acknowledged, though again eros and agape share many features. If agape gives itself away, then so does eros. Eros, too, is directed towards the other, surrenders itself; and to some degree agape also wants to gain by preserving life, approaching it passionately and showing teeth to the powerful who play with the lives of others. There is passionate agape and tender eros. We have to recognize both similarities and differences, for if we ignore the differences, we trigger off the destructive powers of both. Only with one another (though this does not mean in harmony) or against one another (though that is not as an alternative) can both develop.[34]

Paul Avis discerns not so much a dialectic as a complementarity of agape and eros in marriage where the result of sexual union in the birth of children and in release and well-being 'is the clearest sign of the eros of God working through creatures to bring about his good pleasure'. Here agape and eros 'become fused and impossible to separate out'.[35] But Avis still thinks in rather Augustinian terms of libido transcended by eros, and eros in turn by agape.

If we seek to hold eros and agape together dialectically, then we must do so in terms of the relation of individual to society. It is eros which is responsible for the propagation of the species, which lies behind the creation of the small and intimate units of society in which children are reared and find their identity, and learn traditions and values. But such small units (not necessarily 'nuclear families' as we conventionally understand them) only exist within much larger structures – the populations of villages, towns and cities, and the administrations of governments. It is agape which works to make these larger structures just and creative environments within which eros can flourish. Eros is about the celebration of life: of the beauty of the body and of sexuality, of the relationships of women and men and of parents and children, but it is the agape which can be crucified that calls into being a world where such celebration can take place.

Agape versus Eros, or the Spirit of God active in both, in the upward movement and the downward, in response to the unlovely and in response to beauty, in spite of the flesh and through the flesh? The 'in spite of the flesh' of Isaiah 53 is, granted, supremely important in a culture which idolizes youth and beauty, and whose supreme goals are pleasure and happiness. But those theologians who have denied God in the flesh have been commanding the sea to go back, have been committing the sin against the Spirit of calling good evil, of not rejoicing in the good creation of the good God. Both Judaism and Islam have been more clear-sighted here. The Spirit is known in what makes for love, wholeness, truth and freedom. All of these can be denied in the sexual experience, but they can also be found, and in the finding it is God himself who finds us.

7

Spirit and Art

'You shall not make for yourself a graven image, or any likeness of anything that is in heaven above, or that is in the earth beneath, or that is in the water under the earth; you shall not bow down before them or serve them' (Exod. 20.4). Whilst music, dance and poetry played a significant part in Israel's life, there was always more question about the visual arts, though a little later in Exodus the Priestly redactors of the time of the exile felt no inconsistency in ascribing inspiration by the Spirit of God to those who decorated the Temple:

The Lord said to Moses, 'See, I have called by name Bezalel, the son of Uri, son of Hur, of the tribe of Judah; and I have filled him with the Spirit of God, with ability and intelligence, with knowledge and all craftsmanship, to devise artistic designs, to work in gold, silver and bronze, in cutting stones for setting, and in carving wood, for work in every craft. And behold, I have appointed with him Oholiab, the son of Ahisamach, of the tribe of Dan; and I have given to all able men ability, that they may make all I have commanded you: the tent of meeting, and the ark of the testimony, and the mercy seat that is thereon and all the furnishings of the tent . . . (Exod. 31.1–7).

The passage is isolated, and it is part of the familiar contrast between Greece and Israel that one gave rise to an aesthetic and the other did not. Artistic ability is attributed to the Spirit here in the same way as the charisms of the judges: it represents the marvelling of the ungifted person who 'cannot draw to save their life' at the person who can, what was much later celebrated in the cult of genius. But the connection between Spirit and art is far deeper than this. Fundamentally it is that the Spirit is the Spirit of truth and that, as Barth put it, God is the most beautiful of the objects of human contemplation. It is this which is suggested by John's language about glorification:

> When the Spirit of truth comes, he will guide you into all truth; for he will not speak on his own authority, but whatever he hears he will speak, and he will declare to you the things that are to come. He will glorify me, for he will take what is mine and declare it to you (John 16.13f.).

What John calls 'glorification' is the manifestation of the inner radiance of truth, and this inner radiance is, as we shall argue, what we really mean by beauty. What we know as 'art' is the discourse which strives to represent truth as beauty.

Spirit, truth and art

'Spirit' is the name we use to talk about God active in, which is to say fashioning, giving form to, his creation. The name for this activity as it bears on human beings is 'sanctification', which is the forming of the human person into the image of Christ. With Paul, in Romans 8, and with Alexandrian theology, we can view this giving of form less anthropocentrically and extend 'divinization', again a forming, to all created reality. Likewise John's description of the Spirit's work as 'leading into all truth' must not be understood purely conceptually, but covers the fashioning of history in all the profoundest areas of human life: religion, politics, philosophy, science and art. The Spirit's giving form in all these areas is experienced as the search for truth. There are not two processes: a divine leading, and an autonomous human quest. Rather, the divine leading takes the form of the human quest, even though the two cannot simply be identified. The name we give for the impossibility of a simple identification is 'sin'.

'Art is the giving of form, and form alone makes a product into a work of art' (Ernst Fischer). To make this more precise, it is *giving form as the question of truth*: without that question there is no genuine art but only decoration and entertainment. The priority of the question of truth was stated epigrammatically by Eric Gill in his motto: 'Look after Goodness and Truth, and Beauty will look after herself' (where 'beauty' is identified rather contentiously with art). This priority has been latent in the Western tradition at least since Plato banished 'amusement art' from the Republic and kept only what was edifying.[1] Kant judged that where the fine arts were not brought into combination with moral ideas and used only for enjoyment then they 'render the soul dull, the object in the course of time distasteful, and the mind dissatisfied with itself and ill-humoured, owing to a consciousness that in the judgement of reason its disposition is perverse'.[2] Hegel, too, insisted on the fullest identification between art and the pursuit of Truth. According to him art in its highest perfection, 'provides the form of exposition which gives the most adequate account of the content of Truth'.[3] This was not to endorse didactic art, which he saw was more or less a contradiction in terms, but to say that *in itself*, as a product of self-conscious Spirit, and therefore, in his scheme of things, necessarily an expression of much greater beauty than the beauty of nature, art was the 'first teacher of peoples'.

One of Plato's most distinguished contemporary disciples, Iris Murdoch, makes a passionate plea for this position in *The Sovereignty of Good*. With Simone Weil she finds the root of virtue in attention, and art is born of that rigorous *attention* which enables us to see the real beyond the dense obfuscation of self-interested fantasy.

Art, then, is the struggle for truth through form where 'form' means the spiritual structure of the world. A good example of form in this sense is Barth's famous account of Mozart, who 'heard the whole world of creation enveloped by light':

He had heard, and causes those who have ears to hear, even today, what we shall not see until the end of time – the whole context of providence. As though in the light of this end, he heard the harmony of creation to which the shadow also belongs but in which the shadow is not darkness, deficiency is not defeat, sadness cannot become despair, trouble cannot degenerate into tragedy and infinite melancholy is not ultimately forced to claim undisputed sway . . . He heard concretely, and therefore his compositions were and are total music . . . He neither needed nor desired to express or represent himself, his vitality, sorrow, piety, or any programme. He was remarkably free from the mania for self-expression. He simply offered himself as the agent by which little bits of horn, metal and catgut could serve as the voices of creation . . . he himself was only an ear for this music, and its mediator to other ears . . .

To talk of the 'spiritual structure' of reality is to suggest that the question of truth, of how things really are, can be put to the *world* as opposed simply to human consciousness, to suggest that we are not simply left with phenomena, and the ordering structures of our own minds. The possibility of art, as distinct from philosophy and science, implies that the question can be *answered* in terms of the discernment and giving of form. Umberto Eco has argued that Aquinas understood form as the 'structural principle in things', 'the actualizing principle of substance', the way in which the proportion, integrity and clarity of being inter-relate.[5] From this perspective we can say that art is the attempt to discern the inter-relationship of the proportion, integrity and clarity of being. This is what Rilke meant by saying that Cézanne did not paint 'I like it', but 'There it is' (just as Mozart did not write 'this is how I feel' but 'this is how it is').[6] The painter often feels as if the world is looking at him, rather than the other way around, said Paul Klee. He or she is penetrated by the universe rather than seeking to penetrate it. For this reason Merleau-Ponty believed we should take the idea of 'inspiration' literally:

There really is inspiration and expiration of Being, action and passion so slightly discernible that it becomes impossible to distinguish between what sees and what is seen, what paints and what is painted.

It can be said that a human is born at the instant when something that was only virtually visible, inside the mother's body, becomes at one and the same time visible for itself and for us. The painter's vision is a continued birth.[7]

This vision is of form, the 'spiritual structure of the world'. This is precisely not a Platonic attempt to go beyond form to truth, but rather the intuiting of depth *as form*. This is absolutely essential to any theology of incarnation, and therefore to an understanding of where the Spirit of Christ might be encountered. When understood like this, form can only be re-presented as an act of interpretation. Rendering a good likeness to nature may be involved in the representation of art but the two are not identical, a truth which both music and pottery (which Herbert Read called 'plastic art in its most abstract essence') instantiate.

That truth cannot be equated with lifelikeness can be seen simply by comparing Rembrandt's early and late self-portraits, as we are invited to do by John Berger. The portrait of 1634, showing Rembrandt and his first wife, remains an advertisement for the sitter's good fortune, prestige and wealth, as Renaissance portraits generally were, and shares the heartlessness of this particular genre. In the self-portrait of 1664, however, Rembrandt 'has turned the tradition against itself . . . He is an old man. All has gone except a sense of the question of existence, of existence as a question.'[8] What has intervened, in the thirty years between the two portraits, is Rembrandt's struggle for truth, characterized in his case by a growing intensity of compassion, the outstanding mark of his mature work. 'The great artist sees his objects (and this is true whether they are sad, absurd, repulsive or even evil) in a light of justice and mercy', says Iris Murdoch. But when truth is compassion, what do we mean by the 'beautiful'?

Revelation and beauty

'The sense of beauty is satisfied when we are able to appreciate a unity or harmony of formal relations among our sense-perceptions . . . The sense of pleasurable relations is the sense of beauty; the opposite sense is the sense of ugliness.'[9] As Read knew very well, this will not do, for it is not simply form but form and depth together which constitute the beautiful. Beauty is form when it is self-evidently true, but such 'self-evidence' is our response to the depth of reality *manifested in the form*.

> The form as it appears to us is beautiful only because the delight that it arouses in us is founded upon the fact that, in it, the truth and goodness of the depths of reality itself are manifested and bestowed, and this manifestation and bestowal reveal themselves to us as being something infinitely and inexhaustibly valuable and fascinating.[10]

The interrelationship, indeed the unity, of truth, goodness and beauty was the theme of the Scholastic doctrine of transcendentals, which itself looked back to the discussion in Plato and Aristotle. For Plato authentic being, the world of the Forms, is characterized by unity, truth and goodness, and to the extent that the world we experience participates in the Forms, it too shares these attributes. In the *Symposium* he taught that, beginning from our enrapturement by physical beauty, a person could ascend through recognition of the beauty of the soul to contemplation of absolute beauty, an ascent which is at the same time a search for goodness and schooling in truth (*Symposium* 212c). The Western tradition has largely followed Plato in this identification. Kant recognized that evil people might be aesthetes, but felt that 'an immediate interest in the beauty of nature . . . is always the mark of a good soul'. Furthermore,

> the true propaedeutic for laying the foundations of taste is the development of moral idea and the culture of moral feeling. For only when sensibility is brought into harmony with moral feeling can genuine taste assume a definite unchangeable form.[11]

For Hegel, 'Truth is the complete articulation of reality by thought, in thought; Beauty is the complete articulation of reality by thought, in reality.'[12] Does this mean that, as Keats put it,

> Beauty is Truth,
> and Truth Beauty.
> That is all ye know on earth,
> and all ye need to know?

Hegel faced the fact that the world contains much which is not beautiful and allowed that '*das Unschöne*', the dissonant or unbeautiful, might be incorporated in the ideal if it is significant and expressive.[13] This is the familiar expression of the 'aesthetic' type of theodicy, according to which shadows are needed to enable us to appreciate the light. But are there aspects of reality – say, death camps – which *cannot* be incorporated into this universal chiaroscuro? And if so does this not leave us with an ultimate dualism? John Berger suggests another alternative in his essay 'The White Bird':

> We live – if one follows the biblical sequence of events – after the Fall. In any case, we live in a world of suffering in which evil is rampant, a world whose events do not confirm our Being, a world that has to be resisted. It is in this situation that the aesthetic moment offers hope. That we find a crystal or a poppy beautiful means that we are less alone, that we are more deeply inserted into existence than the course of a single life would lead us to believe . . . All the languages of art have been developed as an attempt to transform the instantaneous into the permanent. Art supposes that beauty is not an exception – is not *in despite of* – but is the basis for an order . . . Art does not imitate nature, it imitates a creation, sometimes to propose an alternative world, sometimes simply to amplify, to confirm, to make social the brief hope offered by nature. Art is an organized response to what nature allows us to glimpse occasionally. Art sets out to transform the potential recognition into an unceasing one. It proclaims man in the hope of receiving a surer reply . . . the transcendental face of art is always a form of prayer.[14]

Both Aquinas and Hegel could adopt aesthetic theodicies because for them beauty necessarily characterized a world which issued from ultimate beauty. Berger, with no such metaphysical guarantees, must take beauty as a sacrament of hope (not a consolation for something known to be irretrievably lost because 'almost anything that consoles us is a fake', as Iris Murdoch puts it). Art is 'prayer' because it is the celebration of this sacrament. 'Prayer consists in attention', says Simone Weil, and art is that attention which strives to see order – which Berger appears to identify with the beautiful here – and to affirm it in the midst of chaos. To identify beauty with order is in some sense to go back to Plato. For him, as Collingwood pointed out, the beauty of anything is what compels us to admire and desire it: '*To kalon* is the proper object of eros, "love" . . . To call a thing beautiful in Greek . . . is simply to call it admirable, or excellent or desirable.'[15] But then Plato went further than this and tried to say *why* things appeared admirable, excellent or desirable in terms of qualities which were intrinsic to them, the measure, form and order they embodied.

In a world where evil, which is to say dis-order, is rampant, however, form and order have to be understood in their aspect as depth. Reality, including humanness, is not simply given for us but has to be continually sought for and salvaged. Art, along with all forms of the search for truth, is part of this salvage operation. So far from being a playful diversion of the human race, 'it is the place of its most fundamental insight' – the place where suffering and sin is faced rather than falsified.[16] If we allow ourselves to say this, we have no option but to go for a form of the *communicatio idiomatum* and speak of art in terms of the gospel and of the gospel in the form of art.

Ernst Fischer finds the deepest roots of art in the quest for wholeness and a world which makes sense.[17] 'Making sense of the world' is what we ultimately mean by 'truth', and it is in this sense that Jesus is 'the truth' (John 14.6), for the claim of faith is that the way which he instantiated makes sense of our life. This way and truth, however, in a world where evil and suffering is as evident as it is necessarily takes the *form* of the crucified Son of Man, and it is only *there*, in *that* image that 'we behold his glory', where 'glory' is the inner shining which characterizes beauty, the manifestation of form's depth.

To speak of 'glory' or 'beauty' in connection with the crucifixion is the most radical definition of beauty in terms of truth. Thus Isaiah 53 understood, as the church has always understood it, to speak of Christ is the foundational text for any Christian aesthetic. The Servant (the Crucified) 'had no form or comeliness that we should look at him, and no beauty that we should desire him' (Isa. 53.2). Precisely this figure is the 'desire of all nations', the figure in whom and through whom we learn the true nature of beauty. It is this which is the real question mark against the possibility of Christian art, rather than the impossibility of portraying the divine through the human as Barth maintained. To allow that beauty might be found in an image of torture is to invite the corruption of vision by sado-masochism. 'Refined sado-masochism can ruin art which is too good to be ruined by the cruder vulgarities of self-indulgence' – a devastating comment on much Christian art.[18]

If we insist on speaking of beauty in connection with the crucifixion (and John's 'We beheld his glory' leaves us no choice), what we are talking about is the transcendence of the humility and forgiveness of God over hatred and destruction. Any 'Crucifixion' ought to depict, not a tortured human being, but divine forgiveness. This illustrates what is meant by depth in form, and it applies to any art. To borrow a metaphor from linguistics we might say that awareness of beauty implies recognition of the 'deep structures' of reality. Thus Constable said that 'the landscape painter must walk in the fields with an humble mind. The art of seeing nature is a thing almost as much to be acquired as the art of reading the Egyptian hieroglyphics.' Even for the most abstract art, pottery, we could characterize depth as the intuiting of those forms which 'bring imagination and intellect into harmony', as Kant suggested. For this to be possible the struggle to *see* the world is presupposed.

To silence and expel self, to contemplate and delineate nature with a clear eye, is not easy and demands a moral discipline . . . The appreciation of beauty in art or nature is . . . a completely adequate entry into (and not just analogy of) the good life, since it *is* the checking of selfishness in the interest of seeing the real.[19]

All art is about revelation; art, in fact, is the only valid form of natural theology. What it seeks to do is to reveal, to lay bare, the structure of the world, to enable us to see 'the stone clean at the heart as on the starting-day', as Edwin Muir puts it. All revelation is displacement, and art seeks to break open the totality of our conventional perceptions, to stop us taking reality for granted, to reawaken the sense of wonder:

> So from the ground we felt that virtue branch
> Through all our veins till we were whole, our wrists
> As fresh and pure as water from a well,
> Our hands made new to handle holy things,
> The source of all our seeing rinsed and cleansed
> Till earth and light and water entering there
> Gave back to us the clear unfallen world.[20]

As Berger puts it, art sometimes proposes an alternative world (as, for example, at 'the moment of Cubism'), but more often it opens our eyes to see the world which is already there. Great art faces the reality of evil and suffering and yet continues to affirm goodness and love as ultimate. As the true form of natural theology it leads us to Christ whose life, death and resurrection have exactly this function. It is if not the only, then at least the most sure and most profound, propaedeutic to the gospel.[21]

The corruption of vision

Great art cannot be immoral. That artists may be is the possibility of bad art. Bad art is essentially dishonest art, art which is untruthful to its own emotions and perceptions. There is a level below this, too, which German calls Kitsch, which stems from a corrupt consciousness, which has perverted the question of truth altogether. Such corruption of consciousness 'is not a recondite sin or a remote calamity which overcomes only an unfortunate or accursed few; it is a constant experience in the life of every artist, and his life is a constant and, on the whole, a successful warfare against it. But this warfare always involves a very present possibility of defeat; and then a certain corruption becomes inveterate.' We can see this, for instance, in the frankly porno-graphic art of the aged Picasso. Collingwood is right to take this with the utmost seriousness:

> Art is not a luxury, and bad art not a thing we can afford to tolerate. To know ourselves is the foundation of all life that develops beyond the merely psychical level of experience . . . In so far as consciousness is corrupted, the very wells of truth are poisoned. Intellect can build nothing firm. Moral ideals are castles in the air. Political and economic systems are mere cobwebs. Even common sanity and bodily health are no longer secure. But corruption of consciousness is the same thing as bad art . . . Bad art, the corrupt consciousness, is the true *radix malorum*.[22]

'Without good art a society dies', says Acastos in Iris Mur-doch's dialogue. What contemporary philosophy opposes as bad art the Judaeo-Christian tradition opposed as idolatry, and for this reason Aquinas denied that an idol could be beautiful.

> When considered in the world of ends as a whole, the idol does not fit harmoniously, but provokes imbalance and disquiet . . . The idol may be beautiful in colour and proportion, but it does not fit in with the harmony of the universe. It stands out like a wrong note. It might be *formosus*, but never *pulcher*.[23]

An idol cannot be beautiful because it sets out to embody human fantasy, and thus like bad art only makes visible 'the assertion of self, the dimming of any reflection of the real world'. This obscuring, or we could also say ideological, function of the idol is the deepest root of the biblical hostility to idolatry. Idols contest the truth. Bad art is a form of idolatry.

Discernment then, or to use Simone Weil's term, attention, is at the heart of both art and the appreciation of art. 'It is a *task* to come to see the world as it is.' For Iris Murdoch, the idea of God is one of the fictions people use to screen themselves from reality. But could it not be that the Spirit of the truth which is the crucified Son of Man, rather than plying us with false consolation, precisely works to generate 'the capacity to love, that is to see', that the liberation of the soul from fantasy demands? *The Sovereignty of Good* is Augustine without grace, or with grace reduced to the relentless disposing of all illusions. But grace is the God without illusions meeting us in our disillusionment and leading us to the Good. The eucharist is a 'means of grace', because it placards the God without illusions in our midst. As such it is a constant invitation to the purification of vision, and therefore to love.

Spirit, form and creation

To create something, says Collingwood, is to make it non-technically, yet consciously and voluntarily. When things are created, as opposed to being made, they are not made as a means to an end; they are not made according to any preconceived plan; and they are not made by imposing a new form upon a given matter. 'Yet they are made deliberately and responsibly, by people who know what they are doing, even though they do not know in advance what is going to come of it.[24] In this sense Collingwood believes human and divine creation resemble each other, and divine creation is only distinguished from human by lacking any kind of prerequisite whatsoever. Creation, he argues, is not giving form, because the form-matter distinction pertains only to craft and the fashioning of means to an end. But aside from the fact that the art-craft distinction cannot be maintained, art is indeed a means to an end, namely discerning the *form* of truth and the Good in the world. To eliminate concern with form is to eliminate art. Theologically the identification of creation with giving form is very ancient. Thus only a very small part of the Priestly creation story (Gen. 1.1–2.4) is concerned with calling into being. It is nearly all concerned with shaping, with giving form, with bringing order out of an original chaos. In the same way, 'Art is an escape from chaos. It is movement ordained in numbers; it is mass confined in measure; it is the indetermination of matter seeking the rhythm of life.'[25]

Form is always the form of a certain content, and the content is primary. This can be illustrated in the rise of Christian art.

> Christian artists had to use old forms in order to present the new content in the most direct way possible, since these forms corresponded to familiar ways of seeing – and the prime concern of early Christians was to make the Christian message widely known, in order to create a new world. Generations of artists had to come and go before a new form corresponding to the new content was found, for new forms are not suddenly created, nor are they introduced by decree – which, incidentally, is also true of new contents. But let us be clear about it; the content, not the form, is always the first to be renewed; it is content that generates form, not vice versa; content comes first, not only in order of importance but also in time, and this applies to nature, to society, and therefore also the arts. Wherever form is more important than content, it will be found that the content is out of date.[26]

By 'content' we mean 'the magnetic centre towards which love naturally moves', which believers call God. The inadequacy of form to content is therefore a perennial problem, as there is never a language adequate to the content and every 'form' is 'a different kind of failure'. And yet how radiant are the forms we do in fact have, and how extraordinary an anticipation of the form we shall become. 'We all, with unveiled face, beholding the glory (i.e. beauty) of the Lord, are being changed into his likeness from one degree of glory (i.e. beauty) to another; for this comes from the Lord who is Spirit' (I Cor. 3.18). This progressive calling from beauty to beauty is God's eliciting of reality's final form, the new creation, and the creativity of human art is our constant response to this eliciting on our path through the valley of the shadow.

8

Spirit and the Feminine

Having looked at the kind of experiences which generate Spirit language or where Spirit language is appropriate, we turn finally to the language we must use of Spirit. More precisely, if we use masculine pronouns to talk of God the Father and the Son, should we use feminine pronouns to talk of the Spirit? The propriety of doing so is often urged on the ground of the many feminine images which are used to speak of God in scripture. God is said to be to Israel as a nursing mother (Isa. 49.15f.), as one who gives birth (Isa. 46.3f.; Deut. 32.18), as a mother who comforts a child (Isa. 66.13; Ps. 131.2). Above all Wisdom is imaged in a feminine way. She is the mediator of creation, a 'master workman' who was 'daily YHWH's delight' (Prov. 8.22f.). She teaches people the way to life, and gives instruction for government (Prov. 8.1f.). According to the Wisdom of Solomon she is the 'mother' of all good things, and mediates salvation (Wisdom 7.12f.). In the New Testament the image of rebirth from the Spirit is maternal (John 3.47), and Jesus uses feminine imagery to speak both of his own concern for Israel (Matt. 23.37f.) and for the kingdom of God (Matt. 13.33; Luke 13.20). In addition, the fact that *ruach* is a feminine noun in Hebrew has suggested the possibility of imaging the Holy Spirit as feminine, and conceiving the Spirit as the bearer or instigator of feminine qualities.

The fact that masculine pronouns for God are overwhelmingly dominant in scripture is partly due to the struggle with a Canaanite mother goddess religion which both legitimated oppression and deified the forces of nature and therefore sexuality. Worship of the forces of nature is not freedom, as D. H. Lawrence thought, but leads to the worship of strength, power and virility and contempt for the weak. 'The victims of Auschwitz died because pagan madness wished to extirpate the light and to rule the world in dark, ecstatic nihilism', wrote Ulrich Simon.[1] This pagan madness was the lineal successor of the madness of the Baal prophets Elijah opposed (I Kings 18). In reaction to this cult, Yahwism hedged the sexual with the profoundest reserve, and this meant excluding the faintest trace of mother goddess religion. The feminine was affirmed through the theology of Wisdom, by imaging the church as feminine, and later by the theology of Mary, but this affirmation mostly remained an afterword in a distortingly patriarchal, and therefore misogynist, culture.

As is well known, Gregory of Nazianzus defended the full divinity of the Holy Spirit by claiming that the full Godhead of the Son had had to be recognized before this could be affirmed. 'You see lights breaking upon us gradually', he writes. In theology we must neither proclaim things too suddenly nor keep them hidden to the end, for the one would be unscientific and the other atheistical (*Or.* 31.27). This principle of the development of doctrine is now applied by feminist theologians to language about God. What was true for the struggle of Israel against Canaan is no longer true for us, they maintain, because there has been what Karl Jaspers called an 'axial shift' in human consciousness and at long last the feminine anima is coming in to its own. Christian theology has no choice but to respond to this because what is emerging is one of the 'deep structures' of God's creation, and in this change of consciousness it is God himself who encounters us.

How, then, are we being led to speak about God? Two crucial questions arise. One is about analogy, and its relation to symbol. The other is about the relation of sex and gender to personhood.

These issues are raised in a particularly interesting way by Leonardo Boff in his book *The Maternal Face of God*.[2]

Boff's argument, a classic example of 'natural theology', arises from the new understanding of sexuality gained through psychology and anthropology. Whilst accepting that cultural determinants constitute a large part of the difference between male and female, the medical evidence he cites points to significant genetic differences between the sexes which extend to cerebral structure. All human beings have both male and female traits, but to be a woman is to have the female trait dominant and vice versa for a man. Each sex and each person has everything that constitutes humanness but not in the same way and to the same extent. This means that neither sex is enough in itself and relationship and reciprocity is essential to human being. To be human is to exist in relation, since identity is given through differentiation. The male and female polarity is part of the dialectical structure of all existence between I and not-I, and ultimately between human beings and God. Boff favours Jung's characterization of male and female attributes in terms of light, time, impulse, power, order, objectivity, reason on the one hand, and darkness, mystery, depth, interiority, feeling, generative force and vitality on the other. The dialogue between these two sets of characteristics, both goes on inside every human being and through the encounter of the sexes.

Boff then applies these anthropological insights to the incarnation. If this is what it is to be human, what does it mean for God to become human? The fact that Jesus is male means, according to Boff, that Jesus' humanity contains the masculine and the feminine in the proportions proper to the male. Through the incarnation the masculine acquires an ultimate divine meaning *directly* whilst the feminine does so only implicitly. But if there has been a full and direct divinization of the masculine in Jesus can we not expect a full and direct divinization of the feminine as well? For God to be 'all in all', the feminine too needs hypostatic union with God. This, he believes, actually occurred, in that the Spirit, to whom everything bound up with life, creativity and generation is attributed in 'the founts of our faith', is hypostatically united with the Virgin Mary. The divinizer of the masculine with the feminine is the Word. The divinizer of the feminine with the masculine is the Spirit.

Thus there is a perfect symmetry between the Adam-Christ and Eve-Mary parallels. Jesus and Mary together translate what it means to say that the human being is the image of God, or alternatively that 'God becomes human'. This in turn reflects back on our understanding of God and enables us to say that as Spirit the eternal feminine exists in God. If we ask why we should accept this doctrine, the answer is in terms of the axiom, *potuit, decuit, ergo fecit* – it was possible, it was fitting, therefore it was the case.

The weakest of Boff's arguments may be dealt with summarily. He maintains that Mary is raised to the level of God in order to engender God, for 'only the divine can beget the divine'. But if that were really the case, we would need an infinite regression back to the start of the human race, and the argument runs aground on the sands of evolution. It illustrates that he is thinking in abstract rather than historical terms.

More importantly, his proposals illustrate very vividly the contemporary confusion about what it is to be human, for specialist evidence does not agree, and eminent psychologists and medical experts may be found to support quite different points of view. Boff's whole case rests on the *distinctness* of the masculine and the feminine, and then on assumptions about the role of the encounter of the sexes in the formation of personality. Appealing likewise to specialist evidence, Paul Avis wants to argue that the existence of male and female traits in all of us establishes a fundamentally androgynous understanding of the human which then makes it possible for a male (but androgynous) saviour to redeem women.[3]

Despite all his emphasis on our coming to be in relation, Boff actually seems to work with a hypostatic or essentialist view of human nature. Is it really the case that both masculine and feminine 'natures' need to be 'hypostatically assumed' for men and women to be redeemed? We have seen earlier that Paul Avis argues that if there is no eros in God then our eros is not

redeemed. But is it the case that for men and women to be
redeemed there must be masculine and feminine in God? We are
persons only as men and women, but does this mean that gender
defines us ultimately? Rather than appeal to the debatable
evidence about androgyny, either in relation to persons, to Christ
or to God, can we not recognize that *personhood* is something
which is worked out in and through sexual relations but which
goes beyond them, so that we praise (or damn) people very often
not as being great males or females but simply as wonderful
people. Features that make a fine or an evil person seem to be
non-gender-specific — like integrity, loyalty, a sense of fun,
concern for truth and justice, selfishness, openness, generosity,
profundity on the one hand, or treachery, insincerity, selfishness
and superficiality on the other — do not relate to the Jungian
archetypes, and even those that supposedly do, such as creativity,
warmth, affection or intelligence, are in fact universally predi-
cated of both sexes. The concepts 'friend' (which Moltmann
proposed as a key to understanding the new community) or
'enemy', 'lover' or 'parent', central as they are to human life and
summing up our deepest responses to another person, are in fact
non-gender-specific. This is indeed a very rough and ready *ad
hominem* argument, but common usage embodies the sense and
perception of human communities over countless centuries.
Where the exact sciences conflict, it may provide a more accurate
guide than they do.

To argue thus is, of course, to follow the method of natural
theology, which I have criticized for leaving us with the status
quo, but it is an argument which is consistent with all forms of
christology, which have never, except in very recent heresies, laid
any special stress on the *maleness* of Jesus. To call Jesus truly
human is rather to speak of his personhood, as Barth does, in
terms of being for God, being for others, being an ordered unity
of body and soul, and not being the slave of time. This gives us an
entirely non-gender-specific account of what it means to be a
person, and it is on the basis of some such account that analogical
talk of God has proceeded.

An analogy posits a certain similarity but an even greater

dissimilarity between two entities, and it is a fundamental rule of theological speech that our talk of God is *analogous*. To call God 'Father' does not mean that he has a beard. It says that there are certain aspects of paternity, such as caring and education, which we need to associate with God. Negatively it warns us against any association of earthly fathers with God. Boff seems curiously to sidestep analogy and to think in terms of some kind of direct correspondence between human and divine being, which is why both masculine and feminine must be taken up into God. If we grant the importance of analogy, however, then it seems that at the present 'turning of the axis' maternal language must be used of God. Avis objects that to try to complement male predicates with female ones is to buy into the present system, which is shaped by patriarchy. Thus if we use language of God as Mother in order to highlight God's compassion, we simply re-affirm sexual stereotypes. But since *all* of our language is shaped by patriarchy the choice is between some language, no matter how damaged, or none at all. Here, too, revelation is displacement, and what has to happen is that the language itself needs to be knocked out of the patriarchal totality and reconstituted just as, for instance, agape and charis (grace) were knocked out of the Hellenistic totality and endowed with new meaning by Paul.

We cannot begin from the beginning. The problem is that theology is 'second-order discourse', parasitic on the first-order discourse of liturgy and practice, and this takes us to the realm of symbols. Rosemary Haughton believes that the way in which symbols work means that the female figure of Wisdom, church or Mary 'will also be linked to pagan goddesses, to the feminine images of the Magna Mater, of fertility, of night, and so on, all of them . . . appearing in dreams and myths at all times'.[4] Feminine symbols have, by and large, been maternal and erotic. Are there specifically feminine symbols and images which will shape our faith and practice, which can be incorporated into liturgy, and which will *not* by a back door lead us to fertility religion? It seems to me that there is at least one, but first I want to answer D. H. Lawrence's question – why not fertility religion? Might not a little fertility religion do 'poor little talkative Christianity' a bit of good?

Raising the question illustrates a glaring weakness in Boff's account. Boff's proposals simply ignore the cross, as we would expect from a classic natural theology.[5] Salvation is mediated through the assumption of human nature into God, through divinization. It is not mediated through the historical path of Jesus' obedience and his option for the kingdom. It is actually the icon of the cross which has stood at the heart of Christian faith. Boff seems to replace this with an almost Gnostic ontology which happens above our heads and consorts ill with liberation theology's emphasis on the decisive significance of the historical. Of course one could speak of Mary's suffering: 'a sword shall pierce your heart also' (Luke 2.35). But the fact is that the 'founts of our faith' are completely silent about this. They are centrally focussed on the cross and resurrection, for the latter of which there is only the most abstract symbol of the 'Chi-Rho'.

As a matter of fact, whilst Christian iconography has been predominantly male, its symbolism has often been rather abstract – one thinks of the symbols of Celtic Christianity, for instance. Of course some theories of non-verbal symbolism would read any symbol whatever in a phallic way, but it is a question how much this reflects our own post-Freudian world view. If Celtic imagery catches the rhythm of the sea and the dance, do we have in turn to understand these as images of the feminine and the erotic?

Avis draws our attention to one symbol which has been exclusively male and which need not be so, and this is the Christian priest or minister. The woman priest is precisely the symbol we need which does not call up all the Jungian archetypes and cannot be explained in terms of them. A woman who presides at the breaking and sharing, who rehearses the story of Jesus' betrayal, who expounds the tradition in the ministry of the word, by exercising the representative role for so long reserved for men, precisely makes the point that gender stereotyping cannot be ultimate. In her own person she makes the point that there is no good reason to exclude women from this role, and that rational or ordering functions do not belong exclusively to men, but to all members of the community. She can be in herself the revelatory force which knocks us out of the patriarchal totality. She functions in the community where there *is no male and female*, as Paul said, because all are friends of Christ. She takes on a task where, in many traditions, liturgical vestments served to universalize the minister, to point away from his or her individuality and therefore gender, and to emphasize his or her representative role.

This is to claim, again, that we may function as *persons* in a way that transcends gender, that we do not have to respond to each other in an erotic way, but that there are varieties of modes of response. As the Greeks did in their distinction between different kinds of love, we can repudiate the hegemony of eros. From this point of view the theology and iconography of Mary, which Boff and Haughton appeal to as a bearer of feminist insights, is of very doubtful help. Countless representations of Mary, and even more of St Anne, function to recall the 'mother goddess', whilst the theology of the immaculate conception and '*virginitas in partu*' (birth without breach of the hymen) actually expressed intensely patrichal views about women. The woman minister does not function as a representative of the eternal feminine, but simply of the people of God, exercising her function by virtue of the 'priesthood of all believers', and this symbol we could and should adopt without delay.

Avis seeks 'a genuinely non-sexist, androgynous way of symbolizing God and the sacred' which will come with the appropriate change of economic conditions.[6] At least the roots of this are available in the tradition. The prohibition of images was part of the campaign against conceiving God as deified fertility and virility. The name YHWH, for instance, I will be who I will be, which is far and away the dominant name for God in the Old Testament, is completely beyond gender, though the reverent translation 'Lord' carries patriarchal overtones. The apophatic tradition, as strong in recent Protestant as in patristic and mediaeval theology, is emphatically non-gendered – the 'Whence of our feeling of absolute dependence', the Wholly Other, the Ground of our Ultimate Concern – but it is difficult to pray to or within these descriptions of God. This applies, too, to otherwise admirable liturgical formulae – reference to God as 'Creator, Sustainer and Revealer', for instance. We need personal language and imagery. Martin Buber proposed that we should always speak of God as 'Du', Thou. The Celtic 'Heart of my own heart' and its analogues is perhaps even better.

Attractive as these proposals are, though, they do not meet the difficulty of trinitarian language, which inescapably speaks of 'Father' and 'Son'. Should we, as it were, add a mother to this group – not the holy Trinity, but, following the Cappadocian analogy, the holy Family? Even to propose it is to see how 'Spirit' has in fact functioned as a corrective on a grossly anthropomorphic way of imaging God, pointing away from real fathers to a completely different realm. We can pray to or within the Trinity: 'Triune Lord of life and light'. We are still left with two masculine and one 'neuter' pronoun. There is no instant answer to this problem: the light dawns gradually, as Gregory Nazianzus said. An interim solution is both to seek non-gendered but personal language to use in liturgy, and also to dare to use the feminine pronoun of God the Spirit. This may represent a feeble concession to the spirit of the age as, for instance, Ellul maintains; but it may represent a proper response to what God is doing. If God is to be found in what makes for freedom, then she, God the Spirit, is to be found in the breakdown of patriarchy and the movement towards the kingdom where there will be no male or female but God will be all in all.

Conclusion

The only theology which is of any use today, said Karl Barth, at the beginning of his career, is a theology of daring. A theology of daring corresponds to a God of daring. Such a theology is in any event required if theology begins with reflection on the life and death of Jesus of Nazareth. If it is true, this story properly calls forth amazement at the inventiveness and the totality of God's self giving. But the incarnation is but the hallmark of what is true from the moment of creation, true of God's continuing engagement as Spirit. This self-giving far outstrips the limits of our religious imagination, for 'it is not by measure that he gives the Spirit' (John 3.34). Mediaeval theology, looking back over its shoulder to Plato, saw God in the 'universals', where beauty, truth and goodness were found. 'Where charity and love are, there is God.' This book has attempted to gloss this dictum in terms of a theology of revelation. When the Paraclete comes, 'he will convince the world concerning sin and righteousness and judgment . . . When the Spirit of truth comes, he will guide you into all truth . . . He will glorify me, for he will take what is mine and declare it to you' (John 16.8, 13, 14). These verses contain the whole of a Christian theology of revelation.

Revelation is what displaces us, in all our totalities, reveals our self-deceptions, and opens the path to the kingdom of Christ. It reveals our self-deceptions: in politics, the empty enthusiasm of messianism; in community, the deification of group solidarity in communalism; in our sexual relationships, the blinding of infatuation; in art, the triviality and insincerity of anything which does not emerge from a rigorous concern for truth. Revelation displaces us, knocking us out of our totalities: in politics, from false convictions about 'realism' which in fact ultimately destroy; in community, from the totalities of racial, sexual or class groups where we find our identity at the expense of others; in sexuality, from the totality of our own ego-dominated world, where others exist for our use and our pleasure; in art, from conventional ways of seeing the world. Finally, revelation leads us always towards the kingdom: in politics, towards an ever greater realization of freedom in community; in community, towards that situation where there is no longer Jew or Greek, slave or free, male or female, but all meet as brothers or sisters of the Son of Man; in sexual relationships, to a celebration and affirmation of the body which is not ultimate and therefore not idolatrous, but which is experienced as praise of the Creator; in art, to the recovery of vision, to seeing the springs of the world as the Creator sees them.

This work of the Spirit is liberated, set in train, through the crucified Jew, Jesus. 'He on whom you see the Spirit descend and remain, this is he who baptizes with the Holy Spirit' says John the Baptist (John 1.33). This baptism with the Spirit may be known in every sphere of human activity. Of course the Spirit is to be found also in religion, but not as the paradigmatic locus of its disclosure, as the place we have to expect to find it before all other. So often the values of community, freedom and love are stifled by religion, rather than promoted. In Blake's vision it was 'priests in black gowns' who were 'binding with briars my joys and desires', whilst the role of religion in communal conflict is writ only too large on the world scene. It is religion, last of all, which knows the breath of the Spirit's renewal. Beyond religious waters the Spirit is known in the call to a greater openness, a greater risk, to run a greater danger. 'Consider him who endured from sinners such hostility against himself, so that you may not grow weary or fainthearted,' wrote the author of Hebrews, rounding off his argument (Heb. 12.3). This 'Consider him', which is the burden of his whole letter, is the basis also of any theology of Spirit, which must always be a call to join Christ 'outside the camp'. It is in those places that the Spirit blows.

NOTES

Introduction

1. David Hume, *An Enquiry Concerning Human Understanding*, ed. Selby Bigge, Clarendon Press 1902, Section X, Part II, p.131.

1. Language about Spirit

1. R. Kipling, 'How the First Letter Was Written', *Just So Stories*, Macmillan 1908.
2. This is, of course, how Barth described Schleiermacher's theology. The fact that it is true illustrates to what an extent Schleiermacher actually succeeded in creating a theology of the Third Article, even though this was far from his explicit intention.
3. F. G. Downing, *Has Christianity a Revelation?*, SCM Press 1964.
4. Cf. James Barr, 'Revelation', in *Hastings' Dictionary of the Bible*, T. & T. Clark 1963, and the material in his *Old and New in Interpretation*, SCM Press 1966.
5. H. M. Rumscheidt, *Revelation and Theology. Analysis of the Barth-Harnack Correspondence of 1923*, Cambridge University Press 1972, p.30.
6. Ibid., p.33.
7. The ontological argument is the odd one out in the pattern of natural theology, in that it purports to operate purely according to the logic of the word 'God'.
8. Cf. P. Bauer in *The Kindness that Kills*, ed. D. Anderson, SPCK 1984.
9. Karl Barth, *Church Dogmatics* II/1, T. & T. Clark 1957, pp.316ff.
10. J. G. Fichte, *Gesammelte Werke*, VI, p.599.
11. H. Wheeler Robinson, *The Christian Experience of the Holy Spirit*, Fontana Books 1962, p.28.
12. Ibid., p.13.
13. Karl Barth, *Church Dogmatics* III/2, T. & T. Clark 1960, p.354.
14. Ibid., pp.365f.
15. M. Buber, *I and Thou*, T. & T. Clark 1970, p.89. I have preferred to keep 'Thou' for Buber's 'Du', departing from W. Kaufmann's translation.

16. G. Hendry, *The Holy Spirit in Christian Theology*, SCM Press 1965, p.115.

2. Tradition and Discernment

1. Karl Barth, *The Word of God and the Word of man*, Hodder 1928, reissued Harper Torchbooks 1957, pp.69–71.
2. R. Jenson, in *Christian Dogmatics*, ed. C. A. Braaten and R. Jenson, Fortress Press 1984, Vol. 2, pp.152f.; L. Newbigin, *The Gospel in a Pluralist Society*, SPCK 1989, p.78.
3. F. Kerr, *Theology after Wittgenstein*, Blackwell 1988, pp. 146f.
4. E. W. Heaton, *The Old Testament Prophets*, Penguin Books 1958, p.46
5. James Barr, *The Bible in the Modern World*, SCM Press 1973; reissued SCM Press and Trinity Press International 1990, p.142.
6. A. MacIntyre, *Whose Justice? Which Rationality?*, Duckworth 1988.
7. G. Lindbeck, *The Nature of Doctrine*, SPCK 1984, p.36.
8. N. K. Gottwald, *The Tribes of Yahweh*, Orbis Books and SCM Press 1980.

3. The Criterion

1. Lesslie Newbigin, *Unfinished Agenda*, WCC and SPCK 1985, p.25.
2. Owen Chadwick, *The Victorian Church*, Vol.1, A. & C. Black 1966, reissued SCM Press 1987, p.389.
3. Walter Kasper, *Jesus the Christ*, Burns and Oates 1976, pp.74, 101.
4. Leonardo Boff, *Jesus Christ, Liberator*, Orbis Books and SPCK 1980, p.98.
5. Kasper, *Jesus the Christ* (n.3), p.68.
6. Boff, *Jesus Christ, Liberator* (n.4), p.239.
7. Kasper, *Jesus the Christ* (n.3), p.119.
8. Boff, *Jesus Chris, Liberator* (n.4), p.113.
9. Cf. Jon Sobrino, *Christology at the Crossroads*, Orbis Books and SCM Press 1978, pp. 259f.
10. Boff, *Jesus Christ, Liberator* (n.4), p.221.
11. The arguments summarized can be found in Lampe's essay in *Christ, Faith and History*, ed. S. W. Sykes and J. P. Clayton, Cambridge University Press 1972, and his *God as Spirit*, Oxford University Press 1977, reissued SCM Press 1983.
12. H. McCabe, *God Matters*, Geoffrey Chapman 1987, pp.54f.
13. Karl Barth, *Church Dogmatics* II/1, T. & T. Clark 1957, pp.312ff.
14. Boff, *Jesus Christ, Liberator* (n.4), p.248.

4. The Spirit and Freedom

1. J. S. Mill, *On Liberty*, Introduction.
2. Thomas Hobbes, *Leviathan*, Part 2, ch. 17.
3. Karl Barth, *Church Dogmatics* II/1, T. & T. Clark 1957, p.303.

4. Ibid., p.313.
5. J. Blunck, in *Dictionary of New Testament Theology*, ed. Colin Brown, Paternoster Press and Eerdmans 1980, p.720.
6. E. R. Norman, *Christianity and the World Order*, Oxford University Press 1979, p.79.
7. 2. R. Jenson, in *Christian Dogmatics*, ed. C. A. Braaten and R. Jenson, Fortress Press 1984, Vol. 2, pp.110.
8. R. J. Bauckham, *The Bible in Politics*, SPCK 1989, p.106.
9. *Pace* J. Ellul, *The Ethics of Freedom*, Eerdmans 1976, pp. 371f.
10. Bauckman, *The Bible in Politics* (n.8), p.111.
11. Ibid.
12. Ellul, *The Ethics of Freedom* (n.9), p.332.
13. In *Concordia Novi as Veteris Testamenti*, Venice 1519, Lib. V, 84, 112, see B. McGinn, *Visions of the End*, Columbia University Press 1979, pp.133f.
14. Jürgen Moltmann, *The Trinity and the Kingdom of God*, SCM Press and Harper and Row 1981, pp.204f.
15. H. Gollwitzer, *Die Revolution des Reich Gottes und die Gesellschaft in Forderungen der Umkher*, Munich 1976, pp.21ff.
16. Ibid., p.407.
17. Ibid., p.416.
18. G. Gutierrez, *The Power of the Poor in History*, Orbis Books and SCM Press 1983.

5. Spirit and Community

1. M. Buber, *I and Thou*, T. & T. Clark 1970, p.80. In the first edition, translated by R. Gregor Smith, the text read, 'of the Thou, that is, of eternal life'.
2. Ibid., p.89.
3. W. Pannenberg, *Anthropology in Theological Context*, T. & T. Clark 1985, p.37.
4. Ibid., p.524.
5. G. Gutiérrez, *The Power of the Poor in History*, Orbis Books and SCM Press 1983, p.95.
6. W. Eichrodt, *Theology of the Old Testament*, Vol.2, SCM Press and Westminster Press 1967, p.265. Earlier comments summarize the discussion on pp.233f.
7. R. P. Carroll, *From Chaos to Covenant*, SCM Press and Crossroad Publishing Company 1981, p.221.
8. According to H.-J. Zobel, 'ḥesed', in *Theological Dictionary of the Old Testament*, ed. G. J. Botterweck and H. Ringgren, Vol.5, Eerdmans 1986, p.51. the concept of ḥesed belongs to the realm of family and clan society; ḥesed and emeth together signify 'God's loyalty and faithfulness to his covenant and covenant people', C. K. Barrett, *The Gospel according to John*, SPCK 1958, p.139.

9. Because Hinduism does not entail such belief-claims, Gandhi maintained that it was the least communal of religions, a claim amply
   disproved by the history of the past fifty years. The claim which underlies
   Hindu communalism is that Hinduism is the original religion of India
   and that no other may take its place.

10. *The Guardian*, 5 March 1989.

11. Dietrich Bonhoeffer, *Life Together*, SCM Press and Harper and Row
    1954, p.15.

12. Ibid., p.18.

13. Ibid., p.19.

14. Ibid., p.24.

15. Jürgen Moltmann, *The Church in the Power of the Spirit*, SCM Press
    and Harper and Row 1977, p.316.

16. This question was formulated for me by Rohini Banaji in response to an
    earlier draft of the chapter, and the following paragraphs are indebted to
    her discussion.

6. *Spirit in the Flesh*

1. A. Nygren, *Agape and Eros*, Vol.1, SPCK 1934, Part 1, p.54.

2. A. Nygren, *Agape and Eros*, Vol.2, SPCK 1939, Part 2, p.258.

3. Ibid., p.282.

4. Ibid., p.442.

5. Augustine, *On Marriage and Concupiscence, ch*. 27.

6. *Rosemary Haughton, The Passionate God*, Geoffrey Chapman 1981,
   p.57.

7. Charles Williams, *The Figure of Beatrice*, Faber 1961, p.188.

8. Bertrand Russell, *Marriage and Morals*, Allen and Unwin 1929, p.36.

9. Coventry Patmore, *The Rod, Root and Flower*, London 1895, p.91.

10. Haughton, *The Passionate God* (n.6), p.172.

11. Paul Avis, *Eros and the Sacred*, SPCK 1989, p.128.

12. Patmore, *The Rod, Root, and Flower* (n.9), pp.201f.

13. From the typescript of 'Outlines of Romantic Theology', ed. Alice
    Hadfield; p.29, due to be published by Eerdmans. Charles Hadfield very
    kindly made the typescript available to me and quotations are by
    permission.

14. Iris Murdoch, *The Sacred and Profane Love Machine*, Chatto and
    Windus 1974, p.72.

15. Haughton, *The Passionate God* (n.6), p.46.

16. Ibid., p.32.

17. Ibid., p.54.

18. Ibid.

19. Charles Williams, *He Came Down from Heaven*, Eerdmans 1984, p.89.

20. Williams, 'Outlines' (n.13), pp.71.

21. Williams, *Beatrice* (n.7), p.231.

22. R. Zachner, *Mysticism Sacred and Profane*, Oxford University Press 1957, pp.151f.
23. C. G. Jung, *Aspects of the Feminine*, London n. d., p.44.
24. Haughton, *The Passionate God* (n.6), p.291.
25. See Susanne Heine, *Christianity and the Goddesses*, SCM Press and Augsburg Publishing House 1988, p.176; S. Lilar, *Aspects of Love in Western Society*, Panther Books 1967, p.234.
26. Karl Barth, *Church Dogmatics* III/4, T. & T. Clark 1957, pp.238.
27. This was put to me by Br. Bernard SSF.
28. Lilar, *Aspects of Love in Western Society* (n.25), pp.165, 189.
29. Murdoch, *Sacred and Profane Love Machine* (n.14), p.261.
30. Lilar, *Aspects of Love in Western Society* (n.25), p.176.
31. Heine, *Christianity and the Goddesses* (n.25), p.63.
32. Ibid., p.72.
33. Ibid., p.70.
34. Ibid., p.73.
35. Avis, *Eros and the Sacred* (n.9), p.126.

7. *Spirit and Art*

1. In *The Principles of Art*, Oxford University Press 1936, pp.46ff., R. G. Collingwood argues convincingly that Plato did not intend to expel all art from the Republic but only art which served amusement, so that he is left 'with that kind of poetry whose chief representative is Pindar'.
2. I. Kant, *Critique of Judgment*, translated by J. C. Meredith, Oxford University Press 1957.
3. Hegel, *Aesthetik* 1, 140, quoted in S. Bungay, *Beauty and Truth*, Oxford University Press 1987.
4. Karl Barth, *Church Dogmatics* III/3, T. & T. Clark 1960, p.298.
5. Umberto Eco, *The Aesthetics of Thomas Aquinas*, Hutchinson 1988, pp.69, 121.
6. Letter to Clara Rilke, 13 October 1907 in *Selected Letters of Rilke*, trans. R. F. C. Hull, 1946.
7. M. Merleau-Ponty, 'Eye and Mind' ('L'oeil et l'esprit') in *Aesthetics*, Oxford University Press 1972, p.63.
8. J. Berger, *Ways of Seeing*, Penguin Books 1972, pp.111f.
9. Herbert Read, *The Meaning of Art*, Faber 1936, p.16.
10. H. Urs von Balthasar, *The Glory of the Lord*, Vol.1. T. & T. Clark 1982, p.118.
11. Kant, *Critique of Judgment* (n.2), p.227; the previous quotation is from p.157.
12. Bungay, *Beauty and Truth* (n.3), pp.42f.
13. Ibid., p.48.
14. John Berger, *The White Bird*, Hogarth Press 1988, pp.8f.

15. Collingwood, *Principles of Art* (n.1), p.38.
16. Murdoch, *Sovereignty of Good*, (n.6), p.73.
17. E. Fischer, *The Necessity of Art*, Penguin Books 1963, p.8.
18. Murdoch, *Sovereignty of Good* (n.6), p.68.
19. Ibid., pp.64f.
20. E. Muir, 'The Transfiguration', *The Collected Poems of Edwin Muir*, Faber & Faber and Oxford University Press, New York 1964.
21. This point may be illustrated by asking what it is in Hinduism which constitutes a propaedeutic for the gospel. In my view it is above all the visible sacramental forms of domestic Hinduism, the expression of form rather than any of the doctrines, or its supposed tolerance, which function in this way.
22. Collingwood, *Principles of Art*, (n.1), p.284.
23. Eco, *The Aesthetics of Thomas Aquinas* (n.5), p.187.
24. Collingwood, *Principles of Art* (n.1), p.129.
25. Read, *The Meaning of Art* (n.9), p.33.
26. Quoted in Fischer, *The Necessity of Art* (n.17), pp. 142f.

8. Spirit and the Feminine

1. Ulrich Simon, *The Theology of Auschwitz*, London 1967, Gollancz 1967, p.88.
2. Leonardo Boff, *Mary. The Maternal Face of God*, Harper and Row 1987.
3. Paul Avis, *Eros and the Sacred*, SPCK1989, pp.26f.
4. Rosemary Haughton, *The Passionate God*, Geoffrey Chapman 1981. p.261.
5. I owe this observation to James McTaggart.
6. Avis, *Eros and the Sacred* (n.3), p.54.

INDEX

Not one female cited!!! (Except Rosemary Haughton & Susan Lilar + Steiner + I murdock)